THAT NAME RINGS A BELL

BY

ANN & ROBIN GREGORY

When the Coronavirus interrupted normal life Ann and Robin read through all her diaries and realized they contained a feast which deserved sharing. "We have known so many interesting people and should like to introduce them to you. Perhaps some may ring a bell for you too."

British Library Cataloguing-in-Publication Data.
A catalogue for this book is available on request from
the British Library.

ISBN: 978-0-9934431-8-3

**THAT NAME RINGS A BELL
is published by ATWP-Arundel
and printed in the UK by
KerryType Ltd. Midhurst GU29 9PX
Cover Design by Robin Gregory**

PERSONALIA

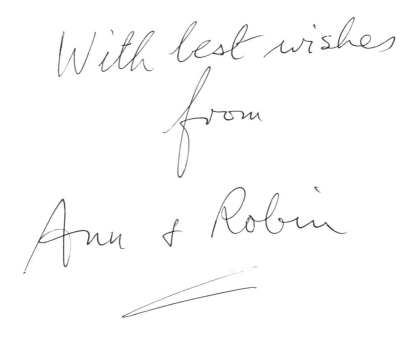

With best wishes from Ann & Robin

The name Portofino rings this bell for Ann Gregory

PART ONE

THE DERBYSHIRE YEARS

Preface: Robin Gregory Reveals All.   Well, almost!

School years are memorable, partly because during those years I
did just once rub shoulders with royalty. It happened this way.
Each year, the school cross-country was held on Epsom Downs,
and my task was to write about the event for the school magazine.
That particular year saw me (by now convinced that a glittering
future as a journalist beckoned) stationed on the Downs planning
where my reporting minions would be placed. While I was entirely
alone, uniformed troops (mainly Canadian) began to assemble, in
tens, in hundreds and ultimately in thousands. None took any
notice of a lone schoolboy watching them get into ranks and files
on the grass. A car then arrived, and King George VI stepped out
to inspect them. I could have touched him, but (of course) chose
not to. I have often wondered how many of those men survived
their European landings. In 1947 India got home rule, and my
father's job in the India Office ceased. While we holidayed in
Dorset, he wrestled with the ghastly prospect of re-locating to the
Ministry of Agriculture, based in Reading. His resettlement
decision also proved decisive for me. I had a year to fill before
university, so I went to Reading School. Two of the school's Old
Boys, the Boulting Brothers, were by then film producers at the
height of their fame and they donated an annual prize to the pupil
whose performance in the school play most impressed them.

1

I played Major Sergius Saranoff in Shaw's *Arms and the Man* ("I never apologise") and although I didn't win the prize, that production cemented my love of theatre.

In the audience was a gorgeous fifteen-year-old from the Abbey School who caught my eye. I'm still married to her! Her maiden name was Ann Elliott: here we are on our wedding day.

Coincidentally, while Ann was gainfully occupying a year between The Abbey and teacher's college ('Gap Years' then did not involve drugs in the Far East), she found herself working in a school where my mother was deputy head. Each admired the other - a good start for a happy family set-up.

Ann Gregory remembers Derek Stanford, 1918–2008

Many poetry-lovers and students of literature know Derek Stanford (*left*) only as the lover of Muriel Spark. For me, however, he was a 'knight in shining armour', bringing enlightenment and salvation as I sought for help in some research I had undertaken on the plays of Christopher Fry.

It was 1951, and I had just seen *The Lady's Not for Burning*, the first of Fry's Seasonal Plays. I had immediately decided that he was the poet/dramatist who should certainly be the subject of my final thesis at college. My own reactions to his wonderful language were strong and favourable, but nowhere could I find published critical analysis. When I wrote to his publishers they were most unhelpful, telling me that I should "write my own essay instead of expecting them to do the work for me."

2

Such reviews as I uncovered all seemed to concentrate not on the play itself but on the performers: that first London cast, for instance, had included Richard Burton, John Gielgud, Pamela Brown and Claire Bloom.

My interested and sympathetic tutor Mr G.B.Thompson came to find me one day, bringing with him a new book by Derek Stanford, *Christopher Fry Album*. It had, apparently been highly praised by reviewers, and not only described Stanford's friendship with Fry during their time in the armed forces in WW2, but also analysed Fry's plays up to and including *The Lady*. I devoured the book and read all of Fry's published plays: my hard work was appreciated and I scored well in my Finals.

My association with Derek Stanford was not, however, destined to end there. In the 1970's my husband Robin created the quarterly poetry magazine *Orbis*. One day, to my great excitement, poems and correspondence arrived from Derek who (unaware of my thesis) indicated that he would like to meet us. Naturally, I could scarcely wait to meet the man whose book had ensured my college success. We invited him and his wife to come and stay with us in Youlgrave and that proved to be the first of many relaxing weekends. On one occasion he gave us a signed copy of his masterly *Inside the Forties*. which mentions many a literary bell-ringing name – including, of course, Muriel Spark.

How I managed, as Head of the village school, to accommodate and cook for all these people I can't imagine now, but the effort was well worthwhile if only for the fascinating interchange of ideas. Derek's wife was a vegetarian, so I always included a fish dish on the menu - her favourite being tuna-fish pie. Derek, very dress-conscious with immaculate casual wear and eye-catching bow-ties, was very figure-aware, and concerned that what he called his 'little pot' might become too obvious. He loved walking by the Derbyshire rivers, and one moonlit summer night when the fireflies were at their best between Youlgrave and Middleton we were enchanted to hear his exposition as to what poetry had meant to him all his life.

For a few years we were working abroad and lost contact. In the 1990s we retired to Eastbourne, just along the coast from his Seaford home and our friendship resumed. We were all, of course, somewhat older, and apart from weekly visits to speak at the City Lit in London Derek had also retired. I often wondered then if he still required an obligatory slice of bread and butter and a glass of juice by his bed in case he woke hungry in the night. Hunger was clearly not a problem when he stayed with us in Derbyshire because the requested victuals were never consumed.

Robin remembers Derek Stanford:

Those Youlgrave years found me editing a poetry magazine, *Orbis*: Derek Stanford 'discovered' *Orbis*, and was a treasure whose literary prose provided many a memorable article. We often travelled from Derbyshire to Cricketfield Road, Seaford where he lived with his second wife, a committed vegetarian. Each Thursday he would set off to lecture at the City Lit - taking in a secret steak en route. They would come to stay with us in the Peak District, where one of our most successful dinner-parties involved Derek (author of a wonderful book on Pre-Raphaelite writers) and Douglas Percy Bliss (former head of Glasgow Art School, and a world authority on Pre-Raphaelite painters). These two stars discovered each other's identity about halfway through the main course; and then all *we* had to do was keep the glasses filled and listen. They agreed on the whereabouts of all the great PRB masterpieces during the war when, despite their decline into obscurity, these paintings had been safely hidden away from London. Derek and Douglas shared tittle-tattle about Rossetti, Burne-Jones and Millais; they talked about 'Bubbles' and his later relatives: oh, if only I had then been able to switch on a tape-recorder!

On a later occasion Derek told us all he knew about Muriel Spark, with whom he had written a book on Emily Brontë. Once their very close relationship came to an end, she spent much of her time belittling his critical abilities; but just try reading their joint book to see who had the more powerful insights.

4

Other of Derek's surprising pieces of information concerned the generosity of Graham Greene and the stinginess of T.S.Eliot when each was asked to help Muriel Spark during a time of financial stress. Derek's amused comment was that this difference changed her from poet to novelist and brought her into the Roman church.

William Alwyn (1905-1985)
Remembered by Robin Gregory

While living in Derbyshire I unwisely published a 'Magazine of the Arts' which I called *Orbis*. The first three quarterly issues lost me a small fortune, because a friend who was in advertising assured me he could secure twenty pages of advertisements, tempting me to a glossy, well-illustrated format. In the event he secured only three pages, which said goodbye to my accumulated teachers' superannuation.

All was not lost, however, as many poets had sent me their poems in the hope of publication and *Orbis* was quickly 're-born' as a simple poetry magazine, soon building up a sufficient circulation to pay its way. I set up a limited company (Hub Publications Ltd), and eventually *Orbis* became the magazine of the International Poetry Society, containing both poetry and articles on poetry. The Society blossomed to the extent that we were able to run a number of residential weekends where members could meet one another. In addition, I began to arrange the publication of chapbooks – collections by a single poet, where the costs were shared, as were any profits.

The great composer William Alwyn came to be a close friend, not because of music, but through my association with *Orbis* and the International Poetry Society (which proved to be one of my happiest achievements). To give the Poetry Society some kind of 'status' I invited a number of distinguished writers to become 'Honorary Fellows'. Their names were well-known to the literati: Kingsley Amis, Sir John Betjeman, David Gascoyne, John Heath-Stubbs (winner of the Queen's Gold Medal for his *Artorius*) and composer Edmund Rubbra, with Christopher Fry designated as

President. I'm delighted to report that *Orbis* is still published today, being now edited by Carol Baldock in Cheshire.

In my time I had several assistant-editors, to whom I gave total freedom. One day one of them (Frederic Vanson) invited composer William Alwyn to 'come on board' and passed me Alwyn's address. I was already a lover of Alwyn's music, so I readily wrote to him with a welcome to our Society. A few days later I received the following reply:

"Lark Rise, Blythburgh, Halesworth, Suffolk
July 28th, 1974
Dear Mr Gregory, Very many thanks for your most kind letter. I am more than pleased to accept your surprising invitation to become an Honorary Fellow of the International Poetry Society. I say 'surprising', as when Frederic mentioned your society to me I thought he was inviting me to become an ordinary subscribing member - which I should have been glad to be. The least I can do is to become an annual subscriber to *Orbis* as well, and if you agree I will send you a cheque. I have read the copy of *Orbis* which you sent with great pleasure and interest. How good it is to come across a 'specialized' publication which is both sane and intelligible! A rarity these days. I particularly enjoyed Harold Hobson's article on the now greatly underrated Christopher Fry. I still remember the delight I had when I went to see the original production of *The Lady's Not for Burning*, and to hear the English language used again with that sense of eternal discovery and joy in words which is our proudest heritage and which is, alas, as much the victim of pollution as the English countryside".

William Alwyn was a shining example of how genius can rise above an unpromising background. He was born in Northampton where his father had inherited a small grocery business. Alone in the family William showed musical interest and, fortunately, his parents proved very supportive.

6

He had attended the local council school but, by the age of fifteen, was attending the Royal Academy of Music studying flute, piano and composition. His father died when William was only eighteen, and this necessitated his leaving the Academy and finding work locally, occasionally as a cinema pianist. [In those days a pianist would play popular music during intervals, for a small fee.] His ability was soon spotted, and he found himself teaching Music and Cricket at a private school in Surrey. A scholarship enabled him to return to the Royal Academy, and his brilliance was such that by twenty-one he was Professor of Composition, and already becoming a renowned international flautist.

He played at the Three Choirs Festival at Hereford when Elgar conducted *Gerontius*, and his *Five Preludes for Orchestra* was conducted by Henry Wood at a Prom Concert. Compositions began to flow from him: fourteen String Quartets, a Violin Concerto and, in 1938, a setting of Blake's *Marriage of Heaven and Hell, a* titanic work for soloists, double-choir, organ and orchestra. With the responsibilities of marriage and two sons he followed the examples of Mahler and Richard Strauss and interwove the intellectual problems of composing with the money-making responsibilities of conducting.

In 1939 he 'disowned' all his existing compositions on the grounds that he was dissatisfied with them, but during WW2 he found a lucrative skill at which he became one of the world's greats: writing music for the movies. In all he wrote about seventy scores for films, including *Alamein* (the theme *Desert Victory*); *Fires Were Started* (a film about the Blitz); *Our Country* (a patriotic film with commentary by Dylan Thomas); *The Way Ahead*, and *The True Glory*. His score for *The*  *Fallen Idol* was a favourite of the critics. After the war two of his most admired scores were for *Odd Man Out* and *The City Speaks*.

WILLIAM ALWYN
THE ART OF FILM MUSIC
Ian Johnson

7

The latter, set in Manchester, brought him into contact with John Barbirolli, who became a champion of Alwyn's music.

As I suspect is a common occurrence, he found a new love in one of his pupils, also a composer: Doreen Carwithen, known to him and her close friends as 'Mary'. Although times were difficult immediately after WW2, William began work on a cycle of four symphonies. This shared with Wagner's *Ring Cycle* the idea of four distinct but linked works. William was disappointed that these symphonies did not get as many airings as he thought they deserved, but his income from film-music enabled him simply to 'hire' the London Philharmonic Orchestra, and to conduct them himself in superb recordings of all four symphonies.

William's ability to write tunes was not appreciated by the powers-that-be at the BBC, but it proved useful when it came to writing scores for films and it was his fame as a composer of film-music that had made him relatively wealthy, allowing him time to follow many new paths: composing operas, for example, in which (being also a lover of the English language) he wrote his own libretti. He was certainly 'multi-talented': he wrote poetry, and translated French poetry into English with great skill. Chatto & Windus published his Anthology of Twentieth Century French Verse.

If I were asked to name his masterpiece I should have no hesitation in saying his opera *Miss Julie*, based on the play by Strindberg. To me this is one of the greatest operas ever written to an English libretto (in this case, Alwyn's own). It was initially broadcast on BBC Radio Three with Vilem Tausky conducting the BBC Concert Orchestra. An LP set of records followed, this time with Tausky conducting the Philharmonia. There is no chorus; just the four principals. The valet, Jean was sung by Benjamin Luxon; Miss Julie was Jill Gomez; Kristin the cook, was Della Jones, and Ulrik the gamekeeper was John Mitchinson. Alwyn knew he had written his masterpiece, as he wrote in a letter to me dated August 4th, 1977: "Oddly enough *Miss Julie* is the first work of mine that, having completed it, I was able to say to myself 'At last a work that satisfies me in every detail. I can't improve on it'.

8

Unusual for me, as everything I have composed so far has always left me with the feeling that if I could start all over again I might do better! I felt in my bones that *Julie* was a masterpiece – but of course this might be due to a senile loss of self-criticism: I have always been my own sternest critic. However I have been flooded with letters from all over the country, including such eminent composers as Lennox Berkeley, Rubbra, etc.,etc. all saying the same thing, so that I am beginning to feel that I am not suffering from self-delusion. One distinguished foreign conductor went so far as to say that Jean & Julie would share a place in the international repertoire with Don José & Carmen, Tosca & Scarpia, etc. It all seems too good to be true."

The tragedy was that he never saw it onstage. I wrote to Lord Harewood who was then in charge of English National Opera. He told me that he received a substantial state subsidy for his chorus, so he dare not perform a work without a chorus. I suggested to George Christie that he should open his brand-new opera-house at Glyndebourne with this English masterpiece. He agreed with my assessment of the work, but said everyone would be looking at the new building rather than the stage so he was planning to present Mozart. So, in 1985, one of my favourite people died disappointed.

In 2020 the work was re-discovered through a fine new radio production but I count myself lucky to have seen the only two stage performances. These took place in Norwich near where Alwyn had lived; and they were financed by his widow. The dates were 15th and 18th October 1997. The servant Jean, the baritone lead, was  Karl Daymond, and Judith Howarth was Miss Julie (*both above*). My great friend Ian Caley was Ulrik the Gamekeeper, and Fiona Kimm was the youthful cook. Astonishing to think that this was a world premiere! Ben Luxon (who had sung Jean on radio and on LP) and Peter Wilson directed. And the Britten Sinfonia was conducted by Nicholas Cleobury. I do have a rather fuzzy video of that performance, but it doesn't live up to my memories.

A jinx seems to hang over *Miss Julie*, however. Karl Daymond, who made numerous appearances in Radio Two's *Friday Night is Music Night* and on Radio Three singing all manner of songs superbly, retired to south Wales, where he conducted the choir. Incensed at the local authority for withdrawing their subsidy he got into such a tizzy that he had a heart-attack and died. Is it perhaps possible that, if there's a special heaven for musicians, he and Alwyn are even now putting together performances of the latter's many songs? I do hope so.

One astonishing truth is that Alwyn and I, though close friends, never actually met face-to-face. A meeting was once all set-up when I was living and working in Lausanne in Switzerland and he was enjoying an annual holiday nearby on Lac Leman at Vevey. His letter of July 16th 1979 made the preliminary arrangements: "Mary and I are planning a holiday in Vevey at the Hotel du Lac, I hope there will be a chance of meeting you sometime between the middle of September and the first week in October." A firm date was fixed, and after a short drive Ann and I presented ourselves at his hotel at the appointed time. I was handed a note. William had, apparently, finally succumbed to the terrible pain of an abscess under a tooth and had been forced to fly back to England for urgent dental treatment. He had tried to ring me without success, and so a tooth had upset all our plans. Just my luck.

John Betjeman, KBE. (1906-1984)

When I started Orbis, the successful poetry magazine linked to the International Poetry Society, I invited John Betjeman to be one of our Fellows. Although I had met him on a couple of occasions when we lived in Berkshire, I had not anticipated that he would even reply to my letter. However, reply he did,  giving me his London address, complimenting me on the success

10

of the magazine, and adding that he was happy to have his name in the list of Fellows. He commented that although he would certainly read each issue, I should not actually ask him to *do* anything. The really important thing was that he had agreed that his name should appear as one of our Fellows.

So, good old J.B., say I. In 1972, when the post of Poet Laureate fell vacant, I was pretty certain that the Queen would endorse *his* name. Despite the odds against him in the press being about 7 to 1 he was, of course, appointed. Alas I hadn't placed my bet so I never made any money out of my judgment,

Christopher Fry (1907-2005)
Remembered by Robin Gregory.

Our first meeting with Christopher Fry (*right*) was unexpected. Once British drama moved into the kitchen (*Look Back in Anger* and all that) Fry slipped from grace. At one time his seasonal plays had attracted the greatest actors but when his wit and verbal beauty went out of fashion, he turned his hand to film-scripts and translations, Anouilh's plays in particular. Summer remained uncelebrated until, years later, Stuart Burge (then doing wonderful work at Nottingham Playhouse) staged the world premiere of *A Yard of Sun*, a glorious summer work set in Siena during the Palio. We were there, of course and with two good friends. As I set off to find four interval ice-creams, I spotted a little man standing at the back, handsome, "brown as a nut" *(Stanford's words)*, and alone. Some instinct told me that this was the author: we spoke, and became lifelong friends. I know of no-one I admire more.

11

In East Grinstead, where we later lived for a while in a Grade One listed boiler-house, I invited Fry to address the local literary society. He accepted, making several things clear, namely that he would speak on the Brontës rather than on his own work, that he would accept no payment, that he would prefer to stay quietly in a hotel rather than in our home "despite Ann's wonderful fish pie" (he had tasted it when we lived in Westminster), and that he would pay for the hotel himself. A fortnight before the lecture, his wife died. He asked to come a couple of weeks later than planned: that was all. Hiding his sorrows, he explained to us all why he thought Anne Brontë the finest of the sisters.

What a disgrace it is that the National Theatre has never staged Fry's whole cycle of four seasonal plays; indeed, I believe that *A Yard of Sun* has had no further stagings since that July 2007 premiere at Nottingham and the subsequent performances at the Old Vic in August 2007.

Christopher Fry (1907–2005)
remembered by Ann Gregory

Although Christopher is mentioned elsewhere in the book, I feel he deserves this personal chapter not least because of his enormous contribution to both poetry and drama during the middle of the twentieth century. Mrs Thatcher's delightfully misquoted reference to perhaps his best-known play ("This Lady's Not for Turning") reminds us of his great success when he was at the height of his powers.

When we first met him in 1970 he was past the zenith of that success following profitable London runs for three of his seasonal plays, each with starry casts. The Spring play, *The Lady's Not for Burning* (1949) had John Gielgud, Richard Burton, Claire Bloom and Pamela Brown. The Autumn play *Venus Observed* (1950) had Laurence Olivier and Denholm Elliott. And the Winter play *The Dark is Light Enough* (1954) had Edith Evans, James Donald and Margaret Johnston.

However, tastes seemed suddenly to change, and the *Kitchen Sink* era took over: The *Theatre of Realism* had arrived with such titles as *Look Back in Anger* (John Osborne, 1956), *The Birthday Party* (Harold Pinter, 1957) and *Roots* (Arnold Wesker, 1958).

Christopher Fry's skill with dramatic words was, however, noted in the United States, which saw in him the archetypal British intellectual: modestly-mannered, grey-haired and tweed-jacketed with leather elbow-patches and a pipe. He was invited to rewrite William Wyler's film-script for the film *Ben Hur*. This led to other similar work on *Barabbas* in 1962, and *The Bible* in 1966. He demonstrated that chaotic film-sets were no problem for an unflappable English gentleman!

At last, on July 11th 1970 the British public got the chance to see Fry's 'missing' seasonal play. Nottingham Playhouse was riding high, following the directorship first of John Neville and then of Stuart Burge. Robin and I were great fans of that welcoming theatre and of Burge's direction, so we made sure we had tickets for *A Yard of Sun*, and we invited two great friends from Robin's RAF days to stay with us and travel with us to the theatre. The stage-setting was July 1946 at the Palio – the exciting horse race that gripped Siena every summer.

Robin has already reported his unexpected meeting with a shortish, tanned, middle-aged man standing in an aisle: "Are you by any chance the author of this wonderful play?" he enquired. "I am", was the reply; and from that moment Christopher and Robin became enduring friends. On discovering that Robin ran the International Poetry Society he sought to be involved – and indeed became President. Later he wrote a wonderful Preface for Czech poet Ondra Lysohorky's *In the Eye of the Storm*.

The Lady's Not for Burning holds special memories for us as, during the 1960s, we played the leads in a production by the Peacock Players, Bakewell. Bob Eaton, then a schoolboy, played Nicholas Devize, and later became the highly regarded Director of Liverpool's Everyman Theatre. We saw *The Lady* again at the Minerva Theatre, Chichester in 2002. Samuel West (he of the beautiful voice) directed, and afterwards we sought him out. He told us that Christopher, now in his 90's and living nearby, had come to see the dress rehearsal and had commented that "we were not making the play dark enough". Sam was fascinated to hear what we had to say about *A Yard of Sun*. Sadly in November 2005 the theatre again resounded to the name Christopher Fry, but this time it was a celebration of his life, as he had died in that very year.

Maurice Carpenter
John Heath-Stubbs, O.B.E. (1918–2006)

Publishing *Orbis* introduced me to a number of eminent writers, many of whom became close friends. Among those was Maurice Carpenter, for whom I arranged the publication of a fine collection of his poems under the title *The Tall Interpreter*. The book was given a lavish treatment by our printers, and to cover the cost we invited subscribers. Over fifty individuals coughed-up, among them John Bayliss, Fred Beake, David Gascoyne, A.E.Gregory (my father), Robin Gregory (his son), Bill Pickard, and Edward Boaden Thomas (author of the titanic *Twelve Parts of Derbyshire*).

Maurice took Ann and me to meet John Heath-Stubbs, winner of the Queen's Gold Medal for Poetry for his brilliant work *Artorius*. I had not realized that he was almost entirely blind, which was probably why the meeting had been arranged to take place in his home where he could find his way about remarkably well. As we discussed one poet's work, for example, he said "Let me show you", and with unerring accuracy he was able to locate the exact book on the right shelf. Some weeks later we travelled with Edward Boaden Thomas, Frederick Vanson and Olive Vanson to a theatre in Essex.

14

An evening's recital was to take place, preceded by a hefty tea. As the time approached when we were to assemble John indicated that he needed to visit the toilet. Much to the amusement of many

THE TALL INTERPRETER

by

MAURICE CARPENTER

With drawings by Gordon Barker

others present, Olive called from one table to another, "Frederic, would you take John to the toilet as he's blind, you see". In every other way the evening was a hit.

As the publisher of *The Tall Interpreter* it was my sad duty to include this note in the book which had started it all:

"When this book was planned, it was to have crowned the work of a living poet. Sadly Maurice Carpenter died on June 4ᵗʰ, 1978. We express our sympathy to his wife, Tina, who prepared the typescript in what proved to be the final weeks of his life."

Lydia Pasternak-Slater, 1902–1989

The very name Pasternak will set several bells ringing. Lydia's father, Leonid Osiporovich Pasternak, was an internationally-known artist – remembered as Russia's first post-Impressionist, and successfully so: in 2004, for instance, his painting *Portrait of Mrs Shalit*, was auctioned at Christies for more than $175,000. He first became popular through his illustrations for Tolstoy's books – published in serial form so therefore requiring a new painting every week. He also made many portraits of his wife and family and, indeed, of himself *(overleaf)*. Lydia's mother was the pianist (and friend of Rachmaninoff) Rozalia (Roza) Isodorovna Kofman.

Lydia's brothers were Boris Pasternak, the poet and author, who eventually achieved fame with his novel Doctor Zhivago – started in 1910 but not finished until 1957; then smuggled out to Italy; translated into English by Lydia, and winning the Nobel Prize for Literature in 1958.

Second brother Alexander Pasternak was an architect: sister Josephine wrote about their father, and looked after his paintings.

In 1921, instability resulting from the October Revolution led Leonid and Roza Pasternak to move to Berlin with their daughters, while the sons stayed in Moscow. Josephine and Lydia studied at the University of Berlin, Lydia changing from medicine, which she had studied at the University of Moscow between 1919 and 1921, to chemistry, physics and botany. In 1926 she received her doctoral degree in chemistry and set about looking for employment.

At the Institute for Psychiatry, Lydia Pasternak had met the British guest scholar Eliot Trevor Oakeshott Slater (1904–1983), a physician and psychologist. She followed him to Great Britain, where they married in 1935 and settled in Oxford. Lydia and Eliot had four children, two boys and two girls, but divorced in 1946. Lydia Pasternak Slater became an important personality in Oxford's literary and artistic society, preserving the memory of father Leonid and his paintings, as well as of the poet brother Boris and his important contributions to Russian literature.

The increasing threat of the Nazis encouraged Leonid, Roza and Josephine to leave Berlin in 1938. They moved to England and settled with daughter Lydia in Oxford.

Ann remembers their first meeting with Lydia Pasternak-Slater: Robin had been in touch with her regarding a book of Lydia's poems and translations then in preparation. Several details needed to be settled, so we drove from Derbyshire to her son's home in the Cotswolds, where she was staying at the time.

16

It was a beautiful hot day, and after ringing the front doorbell we heard a shout from the rear of the house inviting us to come round to the back garden. Lydia was there sunbathing, and she greeted us completely topless. She then conducted the rest of our meeting with no attempt to cover her nakedness. We surmised that this must be quite normal behaviour among Russians, and accordingly we expressed no surprise. We quickly realized that we were dealing with a brilliant woman of strong character who had every confidence in her own ability to make right decisions. Study of her biographical details and pedigree had prepared us for her artistic accomplishments: she was clearly multi-talented.

Her family's political awareness meant that they (like many Russian intellectuals) were forever on the move. Lydia (*right*) had a great advantage over the average British writer in that she was fluent in German, Russian and English. By the 1970's she and most of her family were living in Oxford, and it was there that we met her on several  further occasions. Of some importance was the fact that she chose to attend, and be seriously involved with, a residential Poetry Weekend at Beatrice Webb House near Abinger Hammer in Surrey organised by Robin for members of the International Poetry Society. There were several distinguished writers present, and biographer Derek Stanford gave an outstanding talk on Fry. When Robin invited Lydia to present a paper on a subject of her choice she gave it thought for some days, and then replied, "Would you like me to talk on my meetings with Tolstoy?" Needless to say the answer was a firm "Yes", but we were all a little concerned when we could not locate her as the hour approached. Ever the individualist and sun-worshipper she had booked a taxi to take her for a swim at Brighton; and then to return her in good time to deliver her address. We were impressed by her indomitable spirit. Our last visit to her was to her home in Oxford. On our arrival she confessed that she was due to have a serious operation a couple of days later.

Her doctor had told her she must eat no cream or fatty foods during the 24 hours before the op. She insisted that we join her in eating a delicious cream tea of extravagant proportions about 36 hours before the event "because that may be my last chance for such a feast". What a lady! Having consumed scones and cake, she took us upstairs to her bedroom to view some of her father's paintings. These handsome oils were pulled out from under her bed with little care to ensure no paint chipped off. She stood up several interior scenes and gave us a detailed commentary. "That's my mother and father (*below*).

"That's Rachmaninoff". (*right*).

Astonished at what we were seeing, Robin said "These are superb. They should be in one of our leading London galleries". With a wry smile she said, "I offered them to the Tate, and they just weren't interested." Robin and I lost all confidence in the British powers-that-be that day. What, we thought recently, became of all these treasures?

In 1973 Hub Publications Ltd published a 20-page booklet: *Contemporary Russian Poems, Chosen and presented by Lydia Pasternak Slater*. We remain astonished how well Lydia could take a Russian original and produce an English version which retained the rhythm and the rhyming scheme.

When the 94-page *In the Eye of the Storm* appeared in 1976, among the translations of Ondra Lysohorsky's German, Lachian and Czech masterpieces are no less than four turned into English by Lydia, in the company of W.H.Auden, Isabella Levatin, Hugh McKinley, Ewald Osers and David Gill.

Lydia's voice can be heard if you can run to earth two 7" EPs produced in 1960 by Lyro Record Company. There are twelve poems by Boris Pasternak, translated and read by his sister, Lydia Pasternak Slater.

Douglas Percy Bliss (1900-1984) and Phyllis Dodd (1899–1995)
Remembered by Robin Gregory.

I was offered a post as a lecturer at Matlock Teacher's Training College, and shortly afterwards Ann became Head of the village primary school in Youlgrave, near Bakewell. We lived very happily in Derbyshire for the best part of twenty years.

One of our Poetry Society members lived within reach of us at Windley: he was Douglas Percy Bliss (right), well-known as the former Head of Glasgow School of Art. Not only was he a fine painter: he also had a profound interest in, and knowledge of, English literature. On retirement he and his wife Phyllis Dodd had moved to a lovely house on the edge of the Peak District National Park. There he met another poetry-lover, a retired chemist named Edward Boaden Thomas. Edward had already sought us out in Youlgrave and become a wonderful friend. Indeed, his mighty epic poem *The Twelve Parts of Derbyshire* was initially published by my imprint: Hub Publications Ltd. Edward had introduced Douglas to *Orbis* magazine, to the Poetry Society, and thus to Ann and me. We all soon became very close, visiting one another and sharing full, enjoyable lives.

In retirement Douglas (we never included the 'Percy') played a full part in the cultural life of the area round Windley. He never missed an *Orbis* meeting, and generously included us in some of his activities: each summer, for example, he ran a course on Pre-Renaissance Art based in a monastery in San Gimignano in Tuscany. It was always over-subscribed, so he limited it to lecturers from art colleges and universities. I'm glad to say, however, that he twice found room for Ann and me. I recall that we declined to travel by air to Pisa, preferring to drive in sweltering heat in our non-air-conditioned motor car. We were so sweltering on arrival at the monastery that we each went to our own cell to recover. I stripped naked; and a few minutes later I called "Come in!" to what I assumed was Ann's knock. In fact it was the head of the monastery coming to take details of my passport. "Ah, scusi", he said, and was gone. Apparently he then went next door to see Ann's passport. She assumed the knock came from me, and also said "Come in." She too was naked and received another surprised "Scusi".

Douglas's trips around Tuscany were meticulously organised. He showed us enough treasures to last a lifetime. His two lovely daughters (Pru and Ros) looked after the detailed day-to-day planning, and I recall with special pleasure a trip on a sweltering coach to Assissi.

On arrival we all purchased huge ice-creams, and then enjoyed a preliminary stroll round. I spotted a small notice which announced that the famous Italian soprano Licia Albanese was giving a concert that evening in the very spot where we were to stay. Douglas was amused when, after she had delivered exquisite performances of several Puccini arias, I dashed backstage to speak to her. Her English was perfect: indeed, she was touring with an orchestra from the American university where she then taught.

Douglas always maintained that his wife Phyllis (maiden-name Dodd) was a better painter than he. She specialized in portraiture, and many an ambassador is immortalised by one of her pictures hanging in the appropriate embassy.

Douglas Percy Bliss
(1900-1984)

Phyllis Dodd
(1899-1995)

She asked if Ann and I would 'sit' for her, and it is with the deepest regret that I have to report that foolishly we left it too long, and it never happened.

Perhaps the most intriguing dinner Ann ever served took place in our Youlgrave home in Derbyshire. Staying with us for a few days was Derek Stanford - Christopher Fry's biographer, distinguished critic, former lover of Muriel Spark, and a tower of strength to me on *Orbis*. We invited Douglas and Phyllis to join us for the same meal. As the evening wore on it dawned on both distinguished male guests that they had something in common: the Pre-Raphaelites. Douglas had chosen them as the subject of his opening speech when appointed Head of Glasgow School of Art. Derek was an expert on Pre-Raphaelite poetry, and he had written a book on the subject. All Ann and I had to do was to keep the glasses full, while we eavesdropped on probably the most learned and detailed twosome sharing their great knowledge. They even knew where the greatest of P.R.B. masterpieces had been hidden during the war.

Derek, Douglas and Phyllis are all long-gone now, and we miss them hugely. However Pru and Ros Bliss came to Eastbourne in May 2017 because they had offered several of their parents' pictures to be shown at a special Ravilious commemoration event at the Towner Art Gallery. Ravilious had been at the Royal College of Art with Douglas Bliss, who was an academic as well as a painter, and was responsible for bringing the special Ravilious talent to the world's attention through his many references in sundry journals and books bearing the 'Bliss' stamp. Regrettably my own offer to lecture without charge at this 2017 special Ravilious occasion was declined, and the young females who did speak had no personal knowledge of their subject.

Even in old age Douglas was strikingly handsome, and with a fine head of hair. Heads turned when he walked into a room. No wonder one of Phyllis's portraits of him was entitled simply *Bliss* - an appropriate pun if ever there was. And in the Towner Gallery the finest work on the walls was unquestionably by Phyllis Dodd. Little surprise then, that their daughters Pru and Ros are themselves fine artists, and both have taught and/or lectured on the subject. At Christmas one of our annual joys is that they send a special 'Original' card. Unmistakeable – and signed to boot.

Ondra Lysohorsky (Erwin Goy) (1905–1989)

Robin: Gradually I found myself organising the publication of some substantial books, one of which featured the poetry of a distinguished Czech academic: Erwin Goy, better known by his pen-name Ondra Lysohorsky. This is one of the books in which I take particular pride.

The idea was put to me by David Gill, an academic who wrote explaining how he had compiled a substantial collection of Lysohorsky poems, translated by himself and by such names as W.H.Auden, Isabella Levatin, Hugh McKinley, Ewald Osers and Lydia Pasternak-Slater. I was 'hooked' and invited Christopher Fry to write the Preface. He insisted on reading the entire book, then (satisfied) came up with a preface which is clearly the work of a great poetic dramatist.

Ondra lived in Bratislava, and he invited us to visit him and his family in the summer of 1977. We decided to drive there in our DAF, taking the opportunity to stay over-night in Vienna. From there we took the motorway, and observed that once we had passed the airport we were almost the only car heading towards Czechoslovakia, which was then under Soviet dominion.

The Customs Post was rather disconcerting: we were obliged to change good British coin for the local currency, and were informed that we could use it for purchases but we would not be able to change it back on departure. The Manager with whom we were dealing did drop us a hint that he was "on our side" by offering us a handsome English pen to fill in the several obligatory forms.

All was well, and we drove on to the hotel where Ondra (*left*) had arranged to meet us. He had booked us in for the night, and greeted us in what was to be our room. As we entered he gestured that we should not speak, and then inspected every switch and power-point to ensure the room was not 'bugged'. Satisfied, he asked what language we should speak. Ann told him she had a distinction in German when at school, so off we went in German. "Stop", he said. "Your German is no use." I offered French, having reached French as a subsidiary subject at first-year university level. "Your French is even worse", he said, adding "My first language is Lachian, my second Czech, my third Russian, my fourth German, my fifth French, and my sixth English. So from now on we shall speak English, and you will correct all my mistakes". Rather ashamed, we agreed.

The following day he guided us to his flat. There was no lift, so we struggled up six flights of stairs. On arrival I commented that the flat was rather larger than I expected, and he told us that as a veteran of The Great Patriotic War he was entitled to an extra room. We met his friendly 'partner' (he was a widower) and when, a few days later, the three of us set off to stay with his nephew and his family who lived up near the Polish border, we carried with us a huge picnic which she had prepared. There were many hard-boiled eggs, and, with a smile, Ondra insisted that "all eggs must be eaten".

23

We drove along what passed for a motorway, increasingly aware that the roads left a lot to be desired, and eventually arrived at the nephew's surprisingly large house. He had responsibility for the electrical supply for that northern area, and we were made most welcome by him, his wife and two lovely daughters. Despite the politics we found ourselves falling in love with the area, and still receive Christmas cards from the girls decades later. The nephew asked us to drive the car round to the back so that he could "hide it" explaining that "welcoming a publisher from the capitalist west would not be approved of". And in any case his status was such that he had a sizeable car of his own, and he enjoyed taking us from place to place as Ondra decided what interesting area we should see day-by-day. One particularly interesting trip was to 'the greatest castle in all Moravia'. In one room we were shown the piano on which Liszt had played. Ondra, rather naughtily, told the curator that I was a famous pianist from England, so I was invited to play something. The best I could manage were a few choice chords. Around the roof there were the great names from the past who had been either residents of, or visitors to, the castle. All but one of the names we knew well, so I asked Ondra who the 'famed-unknown' was. He made as if to spit on the ground, then said, "I knew him when he was a leading communist politician. He was not fit that a dog should piss on him, and now he shares a wall with Mozart and Liszt." We all roared with laughter.

Wherever we parked my car we were approached by locals who had never seen anything as modern as that DAF. Communism clearly was not making them wealthy! And Ann was often approached by ladies who would admire her western clothes.

Erwin Goy ['Ondra Lysohorsky' was an invented nom-de-plume which linked a past hero and a mountain] was born in Frydek, a small textile and steel-manufacturing town near the industrial city of Ostrava, which could fairly be compared with Sheffield . He was the ninth-and-last son of a coal-miner, and he was brought up in poverty. At six years of age he contracted infantile-paralysis, but was studious and intelligent, and when he completed a university thesis on Rilke he was awarded a Ph.D.

By 1934 he was writing in his native Lachian, and by 1938 the local composer Leos Janacek was proving another inspiration. When, years later, I told him that Janacek was my favourite opera composer, he dedicated his beautiful poem entitled *Leos Janacek* to me – alas, before the book *In the Eye of the Storm* was published by Hub Publications. Seldom has one individual made such an impression on me. It seemed, as we returned home via Vienna, that we were leaving something of ourselves in Ondra's countryside. When (all alone) he took us to the open-air stage where Janacek's opera *The Cunning Little Vixen* was first heard we clambered to have a photograph to take home with us.

Years later Ann and I were invited to the Czech Embassy to witness Vilem Tausky being given some award or decoration. The Ambassador told me that politics had moved on in Czechoslovakia and Ondra Lysohorsky was now considered one of the country's literary giants. Hadn't we been doubly-blessed! I was so moved by knowing Ondra that I wrote a poem dedicated to him, and take the opportunity to print it here. I should, perhaps, explain that in verse four the 'Irish poet' refers to Hugh McKinley, whose home was on Syros where he edited an English-language paper for distribution in Athens. The 'dramatist by his Sussex Downs' is, of course, Christopher Fry, and one of the 'translators' who fits the description was Lydia Pasternak-Slater.

The White Book
(for Ondra Lysohorsky)

Today I am reading your poems
*   as if for the first time.*
I hold in my hand this white book.
*   Your face regards me.*
This book which I helped to birth
*   Is no longer merely the sharpest fruit on my tree.*
The people and places you speak
*   Are no longer strangers in strange lands.*

Friends were always here:
the Irish poet on his Greek island,
the dramatist by his Sussex downs,
translaters in their Chiltern hills
   or their dreaming Oxford crescents.

But whose was the hand
   laid on the willow wand when the moon was full?
   Who the country lass who brought you mushrooms?
   Who broke into your summer-garden like a storm?

What speaks to me today
Is not the greatness of the minds you've known
But the humanity of the life you lead.

   You speak of Casals not as
   Musician taut with technique
But as one immersed in the rapturous play of a lover.
   Your gratitude is not for his skill
   But for his simple way of loving.

You see Goethe
not in the size of his inspiration
but in the cool wind of noontide,
in the level lawns vivid with sunlight.
in the vines festooning the wall
   of the Frauenplan Garden.

You mourn Auden
Who viewed the future with a saddened mind;
But you recall his letter and his promise (a promise he kept)
To turn to resilient speech
   The words of a Beskidy miner's son.

You hear Janacek (who is now made peculiarly mine)
In the silent people of your Lachian homeland
Treading paths of suffering in the rock
   Which you recall with tears in your eyes.

26

This is the burden of your words:
That for all the depth of your vision,
for all the concern of your observation,
for all your understanding of greatness,
HUMANITY in the truest touchstone.
Here I recognise, across the frontiers
across the hills and waters which divide
not a writer, a sage, a friend of Schweitzer,
But a Man who, like me, eats mushroom and orange,
Likes cats and bright aprons,
Marguerites and wild roses.,

Because I see
The Man like me
Smiling in secret, lying on his back in the grass,
Seagulls expressive of his boldest dreams,
I can better hear the cries you make
the warnings you give,
THE INSIGHTS YOU AFFORD.

L. du Garde Peach OBE (1890-1974)
Remembered by Robin Gregory....

Ann was Head of Youlgrave village school in the Peak National Park for sixteen years, and loved it. We had a period house right in the village and became deeply involved in amateur drama. Nearby Bakewell had a troupe known as the Peacock Players, for whom we both acted (notably as the leads in *The Lady's Not For Burning*) and directed. Ann staged two mammoth spectaculars: *Toad of Toad Hall* and *Under Milk Wood.* I played the King in *Hamlet,* and directed Edward Albee's *A Delicate Balance*, largely because at that time we had a real American in the company to whom I gave the lead. (Ann played an alcoholic.) We all had a good laugh when the local paper's reviewer admired the play as a whole, but commented that it was a pity that, whereas most of the company handled an American accent perfectly, the leading man never got near it.

The climax of our own personal thespian efforts (which included leads in *The Importance of Being Earnest)* came when we won the Ferranti Drama Festival in Manchester playing Napoleon and The Strange Lady in Shaw's *Man of Destiny.* In addition we were introduced to a wonderful old playwright called L. Du Garde Peach who had a private theatre high in the Derbyshire hills where he put on plays of varying quality for three-week runs (including Saturday matinées). The building held about 250, and there was never an empty seat: in fact we found our friends begging for introductions to the ticket-list. There I made what was possibly my silliest gaff. Between the two Saturday performances each week Laurie's wife (a retired skin surgeon) arranged delicious matinée teas. On this occasion I was bewigged in the leading role of Goldoni's *Il Ventaglio (The Fan)* when a tall, elderly stranger came to take tea with us all. No sooner was he settled than he said, "Laurie! Loved yer play. Loved yer actors. Hated yer music." Immediately I felt an urge to defend the translator/director/theatre owner, and, looking the tall stranger in the eye, I said, perhaps a little sarcastically, "Are you an expert on music?" When the tumultuous laughter died down I was told that my verbal sparring partner was organist of Westminster Abbey. I later learnt that he had played for the coronation of Queen Elizabeth II. He took it all very well.

L du Garde Peach remembered by Ann Gregory:

Dr Lawrence du Garde Peach, our good friend 'Laurie', was known to countless young readers and radio listeners as 'L. du Garde Peach' (sometimes interpreted by radio listeners as 'Eldugard Peach'). They remember him as the author of over thirty works in the *Adventures of History* series for *Ladybird Books* between 1957 and 1974, and for his many radio plays from 1924 onwards. He wrote for Punch, for the stage (especially Sheffield Playhouse), and for films.

Laurie's background was formidable. Educated at Manchester Grammar School and Göttingen University, he was a Captain in the army in the Great War (WW1). He later lectured at Exeter University, but his real love was writing. His skill in devising plays for children made him the most-performed playwright on the then (late-twenties) newly-formed Children's Hour on the B.B.C. He progressed to films in the 1930s, devising eye-catching titles such as *The White Sheep of the Family*.

Our first introduction to him, and subsequently to his wife Marianne, came in the 1960's - not through his books, but as a result of the theatre he had founded at Great Hucklow in Derbyshire in 1927. Though he was a great supporter of amateur theatre in general, his own private theatre was by no means run on amateur lines. He always insisted on professional standards, choosing his casts and backstage crews with great care. He was always Producer and Director – and usually Playwright.

We first became aware of his Hucklow Theatre at a dinner party given by the parents of a child who attended my Youlgrave village school. At the theatre we met Marjorie Wildgoose who, as Marjorie Hinckley, had acted at Windsor's famous Theatre Royal. While temporarily at home looking after her young family she was 'spotted' by L du G as 'beautiful, talented and local' - the perfect leading-lady for his translation of Goldoni's *Il Ventaglio* (*The Fan*) which he planned to stage at Hucklow. She was tempted to accept his offer, but was concerned that she might be stuck with an inappropriate leading-man. [we all know how professionals tend to scorn the am-drams!]. During the several courses of a delicious meal she became aware that Robin and I were both members of the Peacock Players in Bakewell, and that my husband had a well-delivered voice. She took note of those facts and some days later suggested to Laurie that Robin might be offered the part. Laurie liked his casts to be of 'the right temperament, character and background' but was not accustomed to accepting someone else's judgment. However, after careful negotiation, it was arranged that Robin and I should be personally 'vetted' by the great man, and we were invited to dinner at L du G's home to 'see if our faces fitted'.

Fortunately we both knew which side to put our knives and forks, and after much pleasant conversation we were accepted as 'suitable for Hucklow'. Robin *(left)* was offered the lead in *The Fan*, and I had a small but enjoyable role. Our host clearly felt it was a good idea to 'employ' married couples, as that contributed to harmonious relationships – and reduced the travel expenses.

Nightly rehearsals over a three-week period were *de rigueur*. We became accustomed to driving the twenty or so miles to and from Hucklow whatever the weather, for three weeks of rehearsals and then three more weeks onstage in front of a full audience. We received expenses for fuel but no fees. Full houses (250 seats) were guaranteed: indeed, so great was the demand that acquaintances attempted to 'bribe' us to secure a seat for themselves. Seats were sold personally by Laurie, and woe-betide anyone who failed to turn-up on their night without letting 'the Boss' know. Since it left an obviously-vacant seat this heinous sin was always noted, and resulted in a refusal for the next production.

The actual building had been associated with lead-mining activities in the area but had been skilfully converted into a Theatre with a comfortable auditorium and luxurious Green Room. Food and drink always seemed to be available, provided by volunteers who enjoyed backstage work and building sets. One memorable stage-effect always caused a gasp from the audience as the doomed ship Mary Celeste appeared to pull out of harbour, rocking and swaying during a storm at sea.

Robin was by then trying his hand at writing plays, and Laurie was generously reading them and commenting.

Sadly Laurie sliced off a toe with his lawn mower and his activities in the theatre were greatly curtailed. We continued our friendship with both Marianne and Laurie until his death in 1974. Many of us would like to have continued to use the theatre, perhaps naming it The Peach Theatre, but his will decreed that the building should be sold and should never again be used as a theatre. In his words "It was my toy, and I don't want anyone else playing with it." In fact, the Boy Scouts benefitted from this instruction as it became their headquarters, and they had many happy years there. The Hucklow Theatre became just a memory.

Brian Asquith (1930–2008)   Remembered by Ann Gregory

Built to commemorate the Millenium, Sheffield's Peace Garden (*above*) is a multi-layered architectural and artistic experience. Its centrepiece is a quarter-circle of huge bronze, lotus-shaped fountains, their water flowing to represent the molten steel associated with the growth of the city's wealth. Surrounding this sculpture are benches, bollards and bins, all complementing the overall design; all contributing to a sense of artistic harmony, and all designed by Brian Asquith.

If, however, you find yourself in the south of England, make sure you visit Chichester Cathedral, where another of Brian's most exquisite creations is to be found. He was commissioned by the Freemasons to create a processional cross, and Brian being Brian realized that if a cross is to be carried it must not be too heavy so he made it of aluminium thinly coated with silver. It was designed to share a place on the high altar with two Asquith-designed candlesticks. Robin and I remember how, quite by chance, we were walking around the Cathedral when we spotted Brian delivering this masterpiece. What none of us realized was that the Cathedral powers-that-be had a dislike of the Masons, and therefore 'hid' the cross in an adjacent small chapel, where no-one would see it unless they asked to be shown it. Robin was so incensed at this that one day he climbed the barrier, setting off the alarms and giving him the chance to make a loud protest! If things are still the same, why not follow suit and complain. That cross is as good as the very best of the cathedral's medieval treasures *and should be on show!*

We first met Brian Asquith (*left*), the designer of this work of art, when he and his family moved to Youlgrave in 1963, a year after our own arrival there. His wife Barbara and I rapidly became friends, and their younger son Jeremy became a pupil at my school. Nicholas, the older son, attended Lady Manners' School in Bakewell. Brian and Barbara bought a large house in the village centre, set up their workshops there, and were quickly absorbed into the local community.

Barbara was a talented designer of her own clothes and, being a beautiful woman, modelled them well. We became regular guests at each other's dinner parties, and I remember that on one occasion she confided in me that she was expecting a third child and hoped it would turn out to be a girl. Six months later, however, Patrick was born and soon became the apple of everyone's eye. Five years later he started at my village school, his inherited charm and talent ensuring a welcome from his fellow pupils and all the staff.

Brian's business went from strength to strength. He received prestigious commissions from the World Tennis Federation, from Royalty, and from the Worshipful Company of Goldsmiths.

He designed and made the cutlery and crockery for British Airways, and was adept at working with specialists at Denby's Pottery where he made the metal components of knives, forks and spoons while <u>Denby</u> made the handles. He also made silver jewellery and, of course, candlesticks for cathedrals. Not at all spoilt by his artistic success, Brian established very strong links with the village. At legendary parties Barbara's culinary skills were much in evidence. And whereas one often assumes that artists are quiet and gentle, both Barbara and Brian were to be seen swimming in the local rivers, even in the coldest weather.

By the 1980's Robin and I were working in Switzerland, living in a lovely apartment in Lausanne. Brian and Barbara came to visit us on several occasions. By then Brian had contracts in Milan with the Italian firm Officina Alessi for whom he was creating a set of tableware inspired by the Victorian designer, Christopher Dresser. We were delighted that he seemed so pleased to share with us details of all his successes.

Even after we moved on from Youlgrave Brian would still find new excitements for us. He introduced us to the Chelsea Arts Club, of which he was a member, and arranged for us to spend a night there with them. He also arranged for Robin to be a guest at a prestigious Livery Dinner at London's Goldsmiths Hall.

Brian told us an astonishing tale of one of his very first commissions. The large NatWest Bank in the centre of Sheffield had paid him a substantial sum for a long wall-sculpture which would relate to Sheffield's link with steel; a sculpture to embellish their otherwise dreary entrance. He confessed that once a year he would go to look at that early commission, and glow with pride until – horror - one year it was gone - the wall was empty and simply painted. He sought out the Manager and asked what had happened to it. "What sculpture?" asked the manager. Assuming he was talking to a new appointee, Brian explained, only to discover that the manager had been there for some years. "That brings one down to size, doesn't it?" he added, "he's passed it hundreds of times and never even noticed it!"

What had happened, apparently, was that the bank was due for decoration, and the sculpture had been sent to the scrapyard. Horrified, Brian then set about tracking it down, and located it at a private scrapyard - still in remarkably good condition. The Yard Manager told him he was studying art at night-school and had recognized something special, so carefully set it aside. Brian asked when it would be convenient to collect it, only to be told that a substantial sum would need to be paid to the Yard Owner, whose property the sculpture now was. Lady Luck was on Brian's side, however, for shortly afterwards he was at a London dinner and had relayed the tale to the guest at his side. It so happened that the fellow-guest was a senior official in NatWest Bank, and he promised that the cost of re-claiming the sculpture would be met by the Bank. He was as good as his word, and the happy ending to this tale is that the sculpture in question now adorns the front elevation of Sheffield's Hallam University where Brian was a Governor.

Later, on retirement, we moved to Eastbourne where Brian and Barbara were frequent visitors. One February we looked out before breakfast and there was Brian heading for the shore to have his daily swim. We warned him that the sea would be very cold, but he laughed and said it would feel like a warm bath after the River Lathkill where he swam daily in Derbyshire when he was at home there.

With his own retirement in view Brian and Barbara bought a beautiful house near Perigueux: the previous owner was one of the Goddards who invented 'Silver-Dip'. The house was approached up a half-mile long drive through thick woods, and had a large swimming-pool, a guestroom, and a workshop: perfect for two artists in retirement. We were fortunate to spend many happy days there, driving via Dover/Calais. The Dordogne is home to a large community of retired Brits, and we met many of their new friends.

Our last visits to them, however, were back in Derbyshire, where they had retained a lovely little riverside cottage at Alport, just down the hill from Youlgrave.

They rented it from the Duke of Rutland, and soon added to its beauty with new sculptures and hangings. They created a gorgeous garden which sloped steeply to the fast-flowing river. We still recall our last visit in 2004, when Brian remained active and was able to show us round a retrospective exhibition of his work in Sheffield, although we noticed then that his memory was failing. After his death in 2008 we continued to visit Barbara and their sons, Patrick, Jeremy and Nicholas.

Neil Ardley (1937–2004):
Recalled by Robin Gregory

Ann and I first met Neil Ardley at the dinner-table of a mutual friend in the tiny Derbyshire hamlet of Windley. At the time Ann and I lived a few miles away in Youlgrave, where we occupied a rented house. We also owned (but did not occupy) a handsome Georgian house in the same village, and I mentioned casually that we intended putting the latter residence on the market. Neil immediately said he would buy it at whatever was the asking price. And, later, he did just that.

He proved to be a delightful neighbour. The house he had purchased had no garage; and as I had built a double-garage at our home, Neil readily took up the offer to share a structure which had cost much sweat and tears at the "We need planning permission from the National Park" stage. We discovered that he and his wife Bridget set questions for *Mastermind*, and that Neil played and composed in the jazz idiom. Indeed, he gave me an LP of his magnificent, symphonic-jazz work called *The Harmony of the Spheres*, which merged his interests in music and science.

Neil was a true polymath. Many an article in one encyclopaedia or another was by him. His daughter was in Ann's school, and proved (unsurprisingly) to be intelligent and free-thinking. Youlgrave had a vigorous social life: Neil played a full part in it.

When we moved to Switzerland, we rather lost touch with him; but he came back into our lives in a strange way some years later. At that time Ann was a Head in Buckinghamshire. The authorities there (unlike Derbyshire) seemed to emerge but rarely from their offices in which they compiled sundry pages of advice for teachers. One warned that a popular science book aimed at children contained practical experiments which could be extremely dangerous, and therefore that this tome by *Neil Ardley* should be avoided. Regrettably he died before we could ask his opinion of this prohibition. I can, however, assure readers that his *Harmony of the Spheres* is entirely safe, utterly brilliant, very hard to obtain but worth the effort.

PART TWO

THE KHASHOGGI YEARS

Ann's Foreword to The Khashoggi Years:
This brief account of five years as Educational Consultants to the Saudi billionaire Adnan Khashoggi (then said to be the richest man in the world) is based on my daily diary entries and is as factually correct as fallible memories allow.

Bearing in mind the differing mores of individual countries and social groups, I have tried to be totally non-judgmental, and I invite readers to share that attitude.

The super-rich of one country may well have more in common with the super-rich of another than with the poor of their own country

The Khashoggi Years:
Our 25th wedding anniversary fell in August 1978, and what could be a better way to wake up than on the luxury yacht *Nefertiti*, cruising the Mediterranean? We had anchored off Sardinia, and a Riva speedboat arrived in the morning to take us and some of the Khashoggi children to the Costa Smeralda Yacht Club for a swim.

A handsome, bronzed, extremely polite gentleman in immaculate swimwear came over to us and invited us to dinner that evening. Naturally we accepted, and after he had departed Robin asked Hussein if he knew the name of the stranger. "Don't you know the Aga Khan?" said Hussein. "We're all invited to his villa tonight." And so it was that, dressed in the best outfits we had with us, we awaited the car that would, presumably, take us to the Aga Khan's home. After a wait of some two hours a fleet of cars drew up on the quayside, then conveyed us, three bodyguards, six Khashoggis, a scantily-clad starlet from a coming James Bond film and six musicians round the coast to our destination.

We were surprised to be eating so late but said nothing. The musicians struck up as we entered, and Adnan called out, "Robin and Ann: can you come here please?" When we were face-to-face with the Begum and the Aga Khan himself, Adnan said "I'd like you to meet Robin and Ann Gregory, my Educational Consultants." Did I imagine it, or was he implying "And that's two things you've not got." We knew the Begum to be a former English fashion-model with three small children, so were happy to respond to her enquiries about 'good schools in England'.

After a sumptuous meal we found ourselves sitting near an English couple who told us they frequently dined there, and then asked "Do you know who these extraordinary guests are?" Robin said, "That's Adnan Khashoggi and some of his family." Her response was "Oh, that explains it Normally the meal is served far earlier, and never have we waited so long as today. But we have heard that the Aga and Mr Khashoggi are jointly planning an extensive development of the Costa Smeralda - and now I know for sure who's going to be the boss."

The Interview:
How did all this come about, and what were the circumstances that led to this summer encounter? Wind back to the January of that same year and you find two people who are very happy with life as it is but nonetheless feel an urge for change and, perhaps, a little excitement. They keep an eye, therefore, on the Times Educational

Supplement, noting especially the opportunities to purchase a school and run it as one feels it *should* be run. Nothing, however, sufficiently appealing for so large a financial commitment - until suddenly, one day, what was *this* advertisement getting at? *"The divorced parents seek to employ a couple to have oversight of the education of their five children. Those appointed will probably have experience of skiing, big game hunting and water-sports, and will be required to live in Switzerland."*

'Live in Switzerland' sounded very attractive. Was this the change of direction we were seeking? Robin wrote a letter politely suggesting that the 'divorced couple' would be better suited if they sought a psychologist and a headmistress rather than a skier and a hunter. That suggestion worked. We were called for a February interview in Wells, where a member of Millfield School staff confirmed that the five children (students at Millfield ranging in age from 5 to 17) were indeed shortly to move en bloc to Switzerland. Intriguingly she added that she was forbidden to tell us the name of our employer, but assured us that we were already shortlisted.

We were very inclined to go no further, but we took the view that one can always back out later whereas one cannot 'back-in' again once one has removed one's name from the list. So it was that in March we were invited to another interview, this time at a house in London's Eaton Square. Here the interviewing board consisted of a very smart, smooth-talking, middle-aged man called Shaheen, a beautiful (so far un-named) woman and a secretary. After initial chit-chat we asked "When shall we be able to meet the parents?" The beautiful woman said, "Oh, I'm the mother", to which Robin responded, "But you're far too young" (which seemed to go down well), and we then learnt that this 'beautiful woman' was an Englishwoman, Sandra Daly who, aged 20, had married Adnan Khashoggi, converted to Islam and taken the name Soraya.

The next question - "When shall we be able to meet the father?" "Well", said Soraya "it so happens that the father is at this moment just round the corner in Roebuck House, Stag Place - and almost magically, a Rolls Royce and driver appeared.

He took us 'just around the corner' to a large apartment where we  were introduced to Adnan Khashoggi, who was between two bodyguards. We recalled reading in the press that he was widely judged to be 'the richest man in the world'. He proved to be likeable and charming, speaking flawless English. He asked our view of 'discipline', and Robin replied that success is achieved when there is self-discipline, the key to all human behaviour. "Are you", he said, "prepared to take the job?" We pointed out that we had not yet met the children, and that they might not take to us. With a snap of his finger he took one of his guards aside and asked him to arrange for us to visit Kenya at Easter, when the whole family would be holidaying there on his ranch. With that, the interview was over.

Kenyan Odyssey:
Life continued in its usual predictable way until the school broke up for the holidays. At 4 pm on Maunday Thursday the phone rang and a voice said "This is Soufian Yassine, about your trip to Kenya. Please be at Heathrow Airport at 8.30 tomorrow morning ready for your flight. Report to the Pan Am desk and ask for Jim Weeks." After selecting what we hoped were suitable clothes we rang a good friend, Alan Wicken (Alan and Robin had been Education Officers together in the R.A.F.) and told him of our predicament. We were up in Derbyshire: Alan lived near Heathrow. When we filled him in on the details he thought we were 'out of our minds', but nonetheless offered accommodation for the night, and added that we could leave our car with him during our foreign trip and (most helpful of all) he would drive us to the airport early the following morning. We really have had some great friends, and Alan was one of the best!

At Heathrow we set about finding the Pan Am desk and Jim Weeks. We were directed to what looked like a cupboard door, banged on it, and Jim Weeks greeted us with "Is that all the luggage you have for a trip to Kenya?" We entered a large room where secretaries seemed hard at work, and Jim said, "I'll just slip out to get details of your flight." Rather concerned, Robin asked which airline we should be travelling on, and was even more concerned when the reply was, "Oh, we don't fly commercial. We have our own planes and pilots." Although Robin had spent three years in the R.A.F. he never felt confident when 'up aloft', so asked "And who's the pilot?" Jim laughed heartly, and replied, "Oh, you don't need to worry about this guy. He used to fly President Kennedy, until Mr Khashoggi offered him more money."

We were escorted to a beautiful Boeing 727. No cramped rows of seats but comfortable armchairs, with facilities which made even the Ritz seem tatty. For example, the taps in the loos were gold-plated. During the flight we enjoyed talking to Adnan's sister, who owned  *Elle* magazine. Eventually we landed in Nairobi, where we were met by two personable couriers, who drove us to our suite in a luxury hotel. What a relief! Alone at last. But our journey was by no means over. After breakfast we were driven to a small landing-field. Our luggage was stowed in a four-seat aircraft, which then took off and skimmed the jungle for about two hours. Suddenly we spotted a swimming-pool with adjacent Harrod's chairs, and a large residence just by the small landing-strip.

Our house-party included Soraya, Mohammed (age 14), Khaled (12), Hussein (8) and Omar (6). A sizeable staff, so we were told, arranged food preparation, organised hunting excursions into the jungle, and so on. The day after our arrival we were asked to dress well as there was to be an important guest: the Kenyan Foreign Minister, with his entourage, his wife and several children. Entertainment had been laid on, and Robin was delighted to be sitting next to the visiting dignitary. "Have you had experience of Kenya before?" he was asked.

Robin replied that when he had been in the Royal Air Force we had lived for a while with a doctor who had written an important document for the government concerning the Mau-Mau troubles. Even as he said it, Robin thought, "Oh I have put my foot in it! This man probably *initiated* the Mau-Mau troubles." Surprise indeed! The Foreign Minister asked "Was that Dr Carothers?" Robin said, "Yes, but how did you know that?" The reply was a welcome surprise: "Oh, as a boy I was at school in England and Dr Carothers was then my school doctor."

This was not to be the only excitement that week. One gorgeous evening Soraya, Robin and I were enjoying a quiet after-dinner drink when a shot rang out from one of the bedrooms. Mohammed and Hussein had been cleaning their guns without realizing that one was loaded. Robin rushed to see what was afoot, and there was Mohammed crawling with blood streaming from one of his legs. First aid was summoned but it soon became evident that he needed proper medical treatment, so drivers and staff took Mohammed off to the nearest hospital in Nanyuki.

We were left in charge of Omar and Hussein, and the keys to the gun-cupboard were thrust into Robin's hand. Hussein excitedly told us that our buildings stood on the path of an elephant-walk, warning us that sometimes elephants would try to reclaim their territory. Fortunately all turned out well, but we could see from these experiences that organization and order were lacking in the family's everyday life, with Soraya a very worried mother. Nonetheless we enjoyed a week of fascinating excursions and leisure, during which Robin wrote a long carefully-worded report which ultimately concluded that we did not feel we could realistically work for so dysfunctional a family, no matter how wealthy they might be.

On our last day in Kenya Adnan returned from his lengthy travels and invited us to report our conclusions after living with the family for a week. Robin explained why we could not take the job: there was no job-description, no hierarchy, no way we could hope to be of use to 'so dysfunctional a family'. Mr Khashoggi cut in: "Ah yes, that's indeed the whole point. And that's why we need you. So now: how soon can you begin?"

I was a Headmistress with summer term about to start: I would need to give three months' notice. "No problem", he said. "Fly over to Lausanne in Switzerland and find yourself a nice apartment. Book it in my name. Then during the weeks before you can be fully available, find ideal schools for the boys and for Nabila. Then simply start when it suits you. I shall pay you a salary during all this time, of course." How could we refuse?

On the Yacht:
By July of that year the boys were safely accepted for Le Rosey School in Rolle as weekly boarders, and Nabila, whom we had yet to meet, had been enrolled as a day girl in Mont Choisi Finishing School in Lausanne.

There was still a summer to enjoy before their school terms began in September - and what a summer we experienced on the yacht *Nefertiti*, chartered by Adnan for his family and friends while his own yacht, to be named *Nabila*, was being built in Italy. Getting to know the family was of primary importance: all four boys were highly intelligent and excellent athletes, although Omar, the youngest, was very worried about his reading skills. How would he fit in to the English 'side' of a Swiss school? He was also missing his Nanny, who had been largely responsible for his upbringing. [His now-divorced mother, Soraya was not with us.]

Escorting the *Nefertiti* on our Mediterranean cruise were several Riva speedboats which, we were told, could convey us ashore for purchases whenever we wished, then bring us back to the yacht. We felt sure that in Monte Carlo we should discover not only a fabulous nightlife, but shops where we might be able to purchase books suitable for the various stages which each of the four sons had reached. We were delighted to find we could indeed buy a whole range of *Ladybird* books, many of which we took back for the yacht's library. Omar was soon a fascinated reader, especially on the subject of those wild animals which he had seen in Kenya.

Among other delights was a visit to Rocci, a sculptor based in Portofino, where we watched in amazement as he made sketches which would later enable him to model the children's heads.

Sailing into Portofino Ann (*above*) had been enchanted by the visual delights of that area. Then, later, when we were anchored off Sardinia we all went ashore to scramble over the rocks. A special high-spot came when we reached Cannes and dropped anchor offshore to view the Son-et-Lumière competitive firework displays, won by Italy with their extraordinary evocation of Italian opera.

By then Nabila had joined us: a beautiful girl, but perhaps lacking a sense of purpose. She sometimes seemed to attract the wrong sorts of friends, and we hoped that the coming English exams at her school would give her something to work for. She was to live with her mother, Soraya, in Lausanne over the next few months. Our accommodation was in an adjoining tower block: a new era for us was about to begin.

Our First Months in Lausanne:

Our apartment could not have been more convenient. Situated on the first floor of a modern tower block in Avenue de Cour, it had three bedrooms, two bathrooms and two living rooms. Soraya and Nanny were in separate similar flats in the neighbouring block, in easy contact. A short car journey took us to Le Rosey school, where we established good relationships regarding our oversight of the four Khashoggi boys. They would spend weekends at home with mother and nanny, and could visit us if they needed any guidance on their school-work. We were, in fact, advisers on any matter under the sun, be it educational, psychological or just a friendly chat. The only feature that made the boys different from other children was their use of drivers and Korean bodyguards, who were always on hand. Mohammed, the eldest, developed an interest in Shakespeare, and did well in his exams. Khalid excelled at sports and won many prizes. Hussein, an all-rounder, enjoyed acting, while Omar preferred the ski-slopes.

We kept AK informed of their progress, and formed a close friendship with Soraya, their mother. Nanny was always on hand and a great ally in decision-making as she had known them all as babies. Nabila, a daily pupil at her finishing school, became a real friend, and would 'pop-in' nearly every day to tell us of her school companions, and asking our advice on various situations which she found difficult to handle. Evenings were often spent with Soraya who loved dining-out and glamorous living. She was a most generous hostess, and when any of our family or friends were visiting from England she would always include them in our outings.

That Christmas the whole entourage, including us, went to Marbella on one of AK's private aircraft. On the flight Robin had an amusing conversation with one of the travelling ladies whom we had not previously met. She revealed that she lived in a Chateau on the River Loire, and Robin said, "How lovely! Do you work there?" "No", she said. "I own it!" In Marbella we spent our time partly in hotels and partly on the yacht in the harbour.

Christmas presents were lavish. Nabila gave me a beautiful Christian Dior dress, and our Christmas tree gifts were Cartier watches. One Christmas party took place at the Roussels who, we discovered, owned the second largest pharmaceutical company in France. In their prestigious establishment up in the mountains (so prestigious that we understood AK was anxious to buy it) we met both James Bonds: Roger Moore, whose children were also at Le Rosey, and Sean Connery - who seemed to me then one of the handsomest men I had ever seen.

One occasion really sticks in my mind. At 5 pm on New Year's Eve Adnan decided that all the ladies in our party should have new dresses. But where to buy them? All the shops were closed. No problem for AK! "Ask them all to open in order to allow his lady guests to visit and choose an outfit to be worn at his party". I chose a beautiful, suitably decorous outfit which was really a little too long for me. "Never mind", said Adnan, "I'm sure it can be altered in time for you to wear it tonight." And indeed, it was. A smiling seamstress knocked on my door at 8.30 pm carrying a suitably-altered dress which I did wear that night. Presumably I was not the only lady who enjoyed such personal treatment. No doubt, when the bill for all this was paid, the shops which gave such wonderful service were very pleased that the yacht had moored there for that New Year!

Joint birthdays in Gstaad:

February 12th is a doubly important day in the calendar, as it happens to be the birthday of two very-much-loved people in my life: Robin, and his father .[Coincidentally, I was also born on *my* father's birthday, January 11th.] What better way to celebrate February 12th than to invite Robin's father for a week's stay with us. Sadly, by then both Robin's mother and my father had died, so we invited my mother to join his father on the flight from England to Switzerland. They certainly enjoyed the excitement of being in Lausanne, but what they had not expected was an unplanned trip to Gstaad.

This was brought about because some minor problem had occurred in the boys' schooling, which needed sorting out while Le Rosey school was in its winter quarters. What should we do, we wondered, about 'mum' and 'dad'? We mentioned our dilemma to Soraya and she immediately came to the rescue, insisting that all five of us should proceed to the fabulous Palace Hotel in Gstaad. We all had a good laugh at the fact that in her haste she had booked only three rooms, forgetting that Mr Gregory and Mrs Elliott were no more than good friends. Such an arrangement might be common on the Continent, but British honour was served by Robin sharing a room with his father, while I shared with my mother.

We travelled to Gstaad on the beautiful little train which passes through such dazzling scenery. Hearing that we were there with Soraya and our two parents, Adnan laid on a birthday party at the hotel. He was a great supporter of the idea of 'family' and enjoyed parties. He was as interested to meet Robin's dad as Bert was to meet him, and hearing that Robin's father had been brought up in West Ham (London) he provided a magnificent cake decorated with footballers in West Ham colours. He really was an employer in a million!

Winter in Switzerland:

During the winter months it was the custom for Le Rosey to move to Gstaad, where the school had accommodation and facilities for both skiing and winter sports while still carrying on the pupils' academic education. This meant that we had to divide our time between Lausanne (where Nabila was still at finishing school) and excursions to Gstaad to liaise with the Le Rosey boys and their staff. Two hotels were used by the Khashoggis: the grand Palace (*right*) and the simpler Christiania.

47

Both featured in our lives during the winter months, though we usually stayed at the Christiania. Generally we travelled there on the delightful little train, but occasionally we drove up in the car.

I recall one occasion when we had gone by train, and Soraya decided to visit the boys. She stayed in the Palace, of course, and asked us to accompany her there. Observing that we did not ourselves ski she nonetheless said we should have ski-wear to convey the right impression, and I was bought a handsome Ungaro outfit which I still use in chilly English winters. It was mid-January and there was a particularly heavy fall of snow: even Gstaad, used to such blizzards, came to a virtual standstill.

Soraya was summoned to England 'on urgent business', which seemed to imply that we should proceed to the small airport of Saanen to fly back to Geneva, and thence home to Lausanne. We were told, however, that Saanen was under several feet of snow, and that no aircraft could take off. "Then sweep it!" she said, and sweep it they did. Our small aircraft took off between two walls of snow. The view was breath-taking, and especially lovely as we followed the Lake to Geneva, landing safely there within the hour.

She was required there and then to pay for the flight, and she produced AK's credit-card, which was accepted. What the 'urgent business' was I know not, but I do know that later that week the newspapers were full of gossip concerning her 'friendship' with Jonathan Aitken, and that a well-known Tory M.P. made a brave statement in Parliament that *he* was the friend in question.

Suffice to say that on one occasion back in Lausanne Robin took a phone-call regarding an assignation when said M.P. flew his light aircraft over for a meeting with Soraya in Switzerland. Interestingly, Soraya returned from that assignation with a cuckoo-clock for my birthday. And about a month later she gave Robin a beautiful leather belt for *his* birthday. The belt was far too large. She had apparently bought a second belt for one of her male 'friends' which was far too small, and so the two belts were judiciously swapped. Robin still wears his on special occasions.

Spring and Summer by Lac Leman:

By now we were able to enjoy the delights of living in Lausanne. Our view over the lake was always interesting as the weather could change from hour to hour, with the mountains sometimes visible, sometimes hidden by thick cloud.

It was on Lac Leman that Byron, the Shelleys and Claire Clairmont rented a villa in May 1816. Although the villa is no longer there,

the Chemin Diodate (*right*) marks the spot. We visited the area, remembering little Allegra, illegitimate daughter of Byron and Claire. She was virtually abandoned, and died in a convent in Italy only six years later. Of course, the Chateau de Chillon still stands by the lake, and is well-known for Byron's *The Prisoner of Chillon* written about that time. Although the whole of Lac Leman is much-loved and very beautiful, the water can still suddenly whip up into violent storms. It was in one such that Shelley (a poor swimmer) nearly lost his life, and it was at Lac Leman that Mary Shelley found inspiration for her famous *Frankenstein*.

Outings with Soraya were always a joy as she was such an unorthodox hostess. We learned never to be surprised at her ability to charm and bewitch anyone with whom she was dealing. On one summer evening we were anticipating a visit to a famous restaurant: Manuel's. Robin was taking five of us in his car (Soraya's secretary and our visiting cousin Alma were also in the party.) He parked right outside the venue. Alas! Manuel's was closed that Sunday evening. However, right next door was another good eaterie which *was* open so we all enjoyed an expensive meal there instead.

49

When Soraya was presented with a substantial bill she handed the head-waiter a credit-card for use next door, at Manuel's, and waited for her receipt. "I'm afraid this card can only be used at Manuel's" said the waiter. I thought Soraya should have been a professional actress as she looked round and said "Oh, I thought this *was* Manuel's. Oh well, never mind, you just send the bill to Manuel's as I'm sure they will sort things out for me". With that, out we all swept, each of us affirming that we too had assumed we were in Manuel's. I can still see in the mind's eye all of us taking leave of a bewildered waiter as the clock struck midnight.

A Near Catastrophe:

Life in Lausanne and Gstaad seemed to be going smoothly. Nabila was happy in her school and continued to visit us for tea and a chat. or perhaps a consultation regarding an essay she was writing. The boys kept up their skills in winter sports in Gstaad, with frequent visits from us. We would stay at the Christiania which provided comfortable accommodation and excellent food. The staff of the school also liked to visit the hotel, which meant that we could get to know them informally over a glass of wine: the best way to discuss any educational or social matters which had arisen.

What could go wrong to disturb this orderly state of affairs? One sudden and unexpected knock on our Lausanne apartment door really put the cat among the pigeons however. A man from the Swiss *Police des Etrangers* asked to see our work-permits. Robin said, "Do we need permits?" "Indeed you do" he said, "and I must ask you to leave the country within a month." This was serious because I had given up a school headship and Robin had severed his links with adult education at the University of Notttingham. It rather sounded as if within a month we'd both be unemployed.

It was therefore fortunate that we had got to know and like Soraya's young male secretary, Rainier Charmay, whose father was a lawyer. Without delay we asked Rainier to get his father to advise if there was any way of settings things on the right track.

He came, he asked details of our employer's names, and he pondered. Within days he came back to tell us he had arranged for the Head of the Police des Étrangers to come to our flat for a discussion about the situation. He pointed out that we should of course be present at that discussion "but you must not join in. In fact you must not even admit that you can speak French. Remain silent, and leave everything to me."

When the Great Day arrived we soon found ourselves feeling very downhearted. The entire conference between our lawyer and the Policeman seemed to be going in quite the wrong direction. After about half an hour we heard our lawyer say (in French) that "Mr and Mrs Gregory will accept your decision, but could you please allow them two, or better still three, months so they have time to arrange for the five children to move to schools in Britain." The

Policeman looked puzzled and said, "Why should the children have to leave a good school like Le Rosey (*left*)?" Our lawyer said, "Because the Gregorys are experts who are paid to oversee their schooling, and if the Gregorys are sent back to England then all the children would have to move there too." There was a moment's silence, then the decision came. We heard from the Policeman, now in perfect English, "Well, we'll see how things go, and I'll see you again about Christmas time when I shall make a firm decision." He tucked his papers under his arm, shook our hands warmly, and was gone. Clearly he had realized that if five of the world's richest children and their entourage were to leave Switzerland, then a lot of money would transfer with them. And the Swiss know about money! We never saw him again.

A Change of Plan:

The beginning of 1980 in Gstaad brought not only family problems but educational problems too.

51

Mohammed was now very keen on Drama and English, and wanted constant talks with us about acting and plays. Hussein and Omar (*left, with Ann and Robin*) also enjoyed coming to see us to talk about the family and to discuss what the future might hold for them. Neither parent, however concerned, was ever there long enough to discuss any matters in depth. We therefore felt we were needed *in loco parentis* for the Spring Term, but how was this to be arranged when we were based in Lausanne? After we had discussed with AK the educational and psychological needs of the children it was decided that more permanent every day access would be better for the family, so local accommodation was sought for us. However, finding somewhere to stay in Gstaad during the season is practically impossible and the only place to be found was a three-bedroom flat attached to the Christiania Hotel, officially at 1,000 Swiss Francs a day although Robin was able to negotiate a reduction to half that figure. With everyone's best interests at heart it was felt that this would provide a secure respite for the boys, and a good meeting-place should any of the school staff wish to consult us. Which they did. A cosy log fire added to the homely feel, and by the end of the week we had moved in. Our new temporary home proved to be a very successful venue for the remainder of the term.

The Korean bodyguards (one is seen here with Hussein and Robin) were keen to learn English, so we added language lessons to our very assorted range of impromptu curricula. So often in our lives we have found that free-ranging discussion is preferable to formal teaching, and we felt that (in spite of the cost) that term in Gstaad was worth the expense.

Autumn and Winter 1979:

Exams were over, the boys and Nabila had done well, and Soraya - needing to move on - had relinquished her Lausanne flat. A beautiful villa in Mougins, inland from Cannes, had been bought for Nabila. *Villa Nabila* was fully-staffed, including a Head Butler receiving an even better salary to work there than he had received when working at the British Embassy in Paris.

Packing for Soraya to go to America was, as you can imagine, a full-scale affair, involving many suitcases. The luxury apartments in Lausanne where she and we lived had been built to a specification demanded by the Swiss government, with cellars (known as 'caves') capable of providing shelter even in the event of an attack by atomic bombs. Unsurprisingly the residents used these caves to store their luggage. When Soraya went to retrieve the cases needed for her American journey she reported to us that her key would not fit any of the cave-doors, so Robin and I joined her below to see what the trouble was.

Down we went, and since Soraya had no clear recollection of where among the fifty or so caves hers was situated. Robin tried a number of doors until, eureka, one opened. Inside were some luxurious white leather suitcases embossed with the words *Princess Radziwill*. The 'successful' key was a cheap affair, and Robin pointed out that it might well fit two or three doors, so we should keep trying. "Certainly not", said Soraya. "I remember now. This is my cave, and if she has been storing her luggage in my place without my permission then I shall take it to the States." Despite our protests a number of white leather cases with the Radziwill monogram travelled to America on a private Khashoggi jet. Whether Princess Radziwill ever retrieved her beautiful cases, we never discovered.

Soon after Nabila had moved into her villa we received a phone call from her. "Could we", she asked, "take time off from the boys to travel to Mougins where she needed advice on sorting out books and equipment for a library she intended to install.

I remember that we drove south from Lausanne until eventually the mist and altitude forced us to stop and telephone for help. Nabila's chauffeur established precisely where we were, and then came to escort us to the villa. What a beautiful dwelling it proved to be. There was a spacious ground floor with sunken seating areas set round a large fireplace. An open staircase took one to the mezzanine floor which overlooked the living area. It was here that she needed help in planning her library and in ordering books (mainly in English). What an imaginative undertaking, with no County Council setting a cap on the total (as often happened during my various head-ships).

Lovely gardens and an outdoor swimming-pool completed the scene, with additional bedrooms overlooking the view. Bertrand, the butler, looked after our every need, and a full staff was always to hand in the kitchen cooking haute-cuisine meals. When we retired to bed there was always a bottle of Champagne by our bedside in case we needed refreshment at any hour. During this stay we really got to know Nabila's thirst for further education, and this was just the start, as we came to understand on many subsequent visits.

Summer 1980, and the Mont Fleury Hotel:

Knowing we were in Lausanne for the summer, many of our friends took the opportunity to visit us during their 'European tours'. We were always pleased to see them, and our flat was accommodating enough to supply bed and board for anyone passing through. Weekends were spent helping Mohammed, who was enjoying English Literature but struggling with Economics.

Hussein was getting to grips with French and Maths, and Omar's  Geography was improving as he studied the voyages of Christopher Columbus, Captain Cook and Shackleton. By July it was time for the usual end-of-term events. The school play, written by the drama teacher, was excellent; and Roger Moore was there to see his daughter give a laudable performance. She had inherited her father's easy manner and good looks. The Von Thyssens were also in the audience admiring their offspring's efforts. Open Day began with lunch in a marquee, followed by prize-giving and speeches. We all wondered why we were late starting, and then realized we were waiting for Mr Khashoggi and his entourage. We were also appalled at the rudeness of the audience while speeches were being made: conversation and comings-and-goings seemed to be par for the course.

With the start of the holiday period Nabila realized it was time to take a more serious look at furthering her education. She discussed this with her father, and plans were made for Robin and me to spend some time in Cannes, staying some of the time at her villa and some at the Mont Fleury Hotel. The three of us could take a serious look at her capabilities and skills, and make plans for her future. Fortunately we had with us a series of tests designed to evaluate intelligence, social adjustment and verbal reasoning, and Nabila seemed to really enjoy completing them. The results gave us a very good idea of how to put our plans to AK.

One amusing incident lent credibility to her results. She had been invited to a splendid occasion in Monte Carlo, and found herself seated next to a handsome, extrovert male. "What did you talk about?" we asked. Nabila replied that she was bored because "he talked about nothing but dancing - dancing, dancing, dancing." "What was his name?" we asked. "Oh, a foreign name", she said, "New, New-something." As the penny dropped I said, "It sounds as if you were talking to Rudolf Nureyev, the most famous dancer in the world." Nabila's comment was illuminating, and pointed the direction for her future education:

"Well, there you are! I've been given all this expensive education yet I know nothing whatsoever about the theatre and the arts. Perhaps you could persuade my father to let me have you all to myself for a while so that you can help me fill in all these terrible gaps." We seized our opportunity with both hands, suggesting that we should take her to London where we could best find music, art and theatre for her to devour. She said we should put the idea to AK, and so it was that we presented our suggestions to him on board his beautiful new yacht, named *Nabila*.

Built in 1980, *Nabila* (*above*) was, at that time, one of the largest yachts in the world. She featured in the James Bond movie *Never Say Never Again* and, under the name *Flying Saucer,* became the villain's super-yacht mobile headquarters. She was also the inspiration for the song *Khashoggi's Ship* on the 1989 album *The Miracle* by rock band Queen. In 1988 Khashoggi sold the yacht to the Sultan of Brunei, who in turn sold her to Donald Trump who renamed her *Trump Princess.* When she was delivered she had five decks, a disco, a cinema with seats for 12, 11 opulent suites, a helipad on top (its funnels were sloped outward to avoid interference with the helicopters), a pool with a water jet on top in front of the heliport, two Riva tenders, a crew of 48, a top speed of 20 knots, and cruising speed of 17.5 knots.

This was the setting for our crucial meeting with Nabila's father. During the discussion we saw Bob Shaheen, AK's No. 2, taking careful notes. At one point Adnan rose from his seat and came to sit cross-legged, gazing up as Robin expounded his ideas. When the session was over and AK had left, Bob said, "Well, you certainly got him hooked.

I've never seen him do <u>that</u> before. I'll give instructions for a suitable base in London to be fixed up, and then I will let you know when everything's ready for you and Nabila to move there."

Autumn in London:

Our apartments could not have been better positioned, with views of Big Ben in one direction and of Buckingham Palace's gardens in the other. We and Nabila had adjoining flats in Roebuck House, Stag Place. We had a driver constantly on hand who could select a 'standard' Rolls Royce or, if we had an extra guest, a 'stretched' Rolls. We also had a white Jaguar 'in case we wished to keep a 'low profile'. We signed for Nabila and the two of us to attend some W.E.A classes. We next contacted an agency which supplied professional tutors, and they sent us a knowledgeable young graduate from Bristol University, Keith Warner, who selected many an opera, ballet and stage-play for us to see.

On one of his visits, Robin (in an entirely unnecessary attempt to reduce AK's expenses) challenged a weekly expense-sheet from the Agency which included expensive taxi-fares. Indignantly, Keith pointed out that he had never used a taxi, and always arrived by bus. Realizing that the invoice was 'milking the rich' we agreed that Keith should 'resign' and then be employed directly by Nabila. She agreed that Keith should receive rather more than hitherto, but that the sum should be below that charged by the Agent. We grew to like Keith, who had recently celebrated his 24th birthday, and happily congratulated him when Lord Harewood offered him a post as resident Producer at English National Opera. We have kept in touch with Keith, attended his wedding and followed his rise to fame. He has since twice directed the entire Wagner Ring Cycle at Covent Garden, and recently directed Samuel Barber's *Vanessa* at Glyndebourne.

Adnan Khashoggi had offices in Roebuck House looking after admin. and finances. The Manager, Mr Challaby, was an astute accountant who kept an eye on our affairs. Just as well, because Nabila would often invite others to join us, especially Khashoggi relatives with bases in London. Our own apartment had a super kitchen where we could cook for ourselves, or enjoy the expertise of Gina, a Portuguese who was personally based there in order that in the event of AK calling at his fine apartment (with or without guests) good, home-cooked food was readily available. We really saw how the super-rich lived when, one day, Nabila showed us her father's shoe-rack - containing 48 pairs of Lobb shoes.

Nabila thoroughly enjoyed our outings to modern plays and musicals (many chosen by Keith), and the truly-English Stanley Spencer exhibition at the Royal Academy. We learnt a lot about the London business-world from a visit to Bridon Hamlyn Accountants. Suddenly, though, we were on the move again: Adnan had given a substantial sum to the Benaki Museum in Athens, which was showing Dr Helen Philon's Exhibition of Islamic ceramics. They invited AK to speak at the opening ceremony, but he declined, suggesting that Nabila should speak instead. She agreed, with the proviso that Robin and I would accompany her to Greece and help with her opening speech. Knowing that the journey would be on the most comfortable of aircraft, we started packing our suitcases.

November 1980 in Greece

November 11th we and Nabila were taken in a black Daimler limousine to Heathrow Airport. Our private DC9 took off at mid-day. We reached Athens 3 hours 12 minutes later. En route we enjoyed lobster thermidor, chicken, and a delicious Greek confection. The inclusion of wine surprised  us. On landing we were joined on the aircraft by the Athens Chief of Police and several other officials, and then were driven to the Hotel Grande Bretagne.

The evening was spent in a typically Greek restaurant to which we had chosen to walk as the weather was so warm and balmy. The next day we were met at 10 a.m. by a hired guide for visits to the Acropolis, the Parthenon and the Archaeology Museum. A car was available, although we did quite a spot of walking too. The afternoon was spent touring various seaside towns. We were most impressed as nowhere did we have to wait, to queue or to pay any fee. In the evening we dined with fifteen Greek dignitaries, all of whom (thankfully) spoke faultless English. Midnight saw us back at our hotel, with heads reeling somewhat after such an action-packed day.

It was clear that the Khashoggi contribution to the imminent Islamic Ceramics exhibition at the Benaki Museum was both considerable and much appreciated. Nabila seemed to be enjoying her ambassadorial duties as her father's nominated deputy, and surprisingly discovered that she would be meeting an old school-friend from Millfield.

The next morning we were whizzed off to the Benaki Museum where the eminent scholar Dr Helen Philon was to speak on her 'special' subject: Islamic Art. Interpreters from Saudi Arabia were there to ensure we all understood her well-chosen words, and Nabila gave a short speech saying how honoured she was to be involved in such an important project. The stunning exhibition was intelligently and artistically displayed. Lunch was in the Tudor Room of the King George Hotel – a superb area with magnificent views of the Acropolis. We were joined by an official from the Greek Embassy and a correspondent from the Financial Times. And that evening we were invited to the lovely home of a famous soprano (no – not Maria Callas) whose name escapes me. Her many servants and lavish life-style were indicative of someone acclaimed in that region.

Our last day was spent shopping, and visiting Hadrian's Arch and the Temple of Jupiter which seemed to have an adjacent little zoo with ducks. Our aircraft was due to take off at 7 p.m., and we were onboard in good time. Champagne and canapes were served by the local police and the Friends of the Benaki Museum.

We assumed we would fly straight to London, but en route the journey was broken for two days in Nice so that Nabila could see her dogs. We seized the brief opportunity to re-visit the Mont Fleury Hotel, where the staff greeted us like long-lost friends, no doubt recalling our long summer stay there.

It's worth commenting that when we landed at Nice, Nabila's driver Dan was waiting for us with his limousine right by the runway so we just got into the car and were gone: never did we see any 'customs'. It was good to be on our own again to reflect on the excitement of the last few days, but we were not sorry to fly on to Heathrow on November 17th. The DC9 was lavish with more champagne and caviar, and we arrived in London to be met by three limousines and, again, no need to pass through 'customs'. Back in London at Roebuck House Gina had prepared a delicious chicken dinner for us, so Nabila, Robin and I tucked in to a good old English meal, during which we discussed all that we had seen during the last few days.

Spring in Mougins at the Villa Nabila:

As we were beginning to learn, the best-laid plans often seem to go awry when working with the Khashoggis. A call from Nabila in January announced with distress that a minor operation had taken place thus preventing her immediate return to London. "Please, please could we go to Mougins – taking any required books." She clearly didn't want any interruption of her studies. We raided Foyles for a selection of English novels, packed the car and set off on the two-day drive. Nabila also wanted advice on a music-room she was setting up, so our presence would be doubly valuable. Her knowledge of classical music was limited, and she wished to have a full range of recorded material available for any visitors. As you can imagine, this was an added bonus to our schedule. Early February is not usually the best time of year to travel to the south of France but we arrived in bright sun. Although Khashoggi transport was always at our disposal we preferred to make our own arrangements and travel in our own car, which gave us a degree of independence.

As always, the Villa was a delight. The music-room was under construction, and our beautiful spacious bedroom overlooked the swimming-pool. Nabila was pleased to see us, and after one of Bertrand's delicious meals we sat talking until late. The next few days were spent discussing D.H.Lawrence and the English novel, and going to Valbonne in convoy with Nabila who was practising

driving her new Fiat X19 accompanied by Arlette (wife of Dan, the chauffeur). In nearby Vallauris, a beautiful place noted for its ceramics, Nabila bought large vases for her villa, and we bought a large umbrella-stand which now resides in our Eastbourne  cloakroom. We were a little worried on the return journey from Valbonne when we lost their car at some traffic-lights, but all was well and they arrived back at the Villa about ten minutes after us.

Yet more excitement was to follow: Nabila told us that her artist friend Debbie Nitke was coming from New York to recover from a depression. She had been told of our visit, and Nabila felt we might be able to help with her recuperation - Nabila always had great faith in our ability to perform miracles, however hard we tried to dissuade her! We promised to help if we could, and collected Debbie from Nice Airport (she had flown in on one of Adnan's private jets) and we were anxious to see how she would respond to Nabila's kindness and concern. It was immediately clear that depression had not affected Debbie's looks or personality. She was

 a striking young lady with flowing hair and a gorgeous smile. Over dinner Debbie (*left, with Adnan and Nabila*) described her concerns that her father had reached that 'certain age' when his attentions were beginning to wander. Her mother, in a desperate attempt

to stay young, had seemingly neglected to perceive the needs of her late-teen-aged daughter: as a result, Debbie had built up feelings of insecurity. We decided that listeners with sympathetic ears were needed, and over the next few days we listened (and watched) as Debbie completed a huge painting of New York by Night. Her technique was fascinating: skilled use of spray-guns allied to rotation of the canvas which dribbled the paint to suggest those right-angled streets in that busy city. Dark reds, blacks and greens seemed to release some of her inner tension and, a few days later, Debbie announced that she felt considerably better.

We felt we should offer to buy her picture (although it was certainly not to our taste) but we feared her price might be beyond us. Two days later we found that Debbie had flown back to New York: propped up outside our bedroom door was her picture, with the following message: "I'd like to thank you guys for all you've done for me. Please accept this picture with my love." That very picture now hangs over the settee in our Eastbourne apartment.

Security, and a Birthday:

One aspect of living in Nabila's beautiful home had never occurred to us until one evening she said, "By the way, if you wish to wander round the garden and pool after dark you <u>must</u> first ring this number." "But why?" we asked. "If you don't, the dogs will think you are burglars and will attack you", she said. Apparently at dusk every evening two men and three large Alsatian dogs arrived by security van and patrolled the outdoor area at intervals to see all was well.
"What would happen if we didn't follow instructions?" we asked. "You would be savaged", was the reply. Not quite believing this would be the case, we expressed incredulity, only to be asked if we would like a demonstration. And a demonstration we were indeed given! Dan, her trusty chauffeur and two of the gardeners agreed to be part of the show. From inside tightly-closed patio-doors we could see everything that was going on as, dressed in thickly-padded leather jackets, trousers and hoods, and carrying guns, the three men climbed over the boundary walls and made their way to

the pool area. Snarling and growling the dogs flew at the approaching 'prowlers', paying particular attention to throats and groins. We needed no more convincing. "Call them off!" we shouted as we realized these canine creatures, so docile in appearance, could be far more convincing than hidden cameras! The 'heroes' were rewarded with sustenance and a stiff drink.

Once again fate decreed that we should spend Robin's birthday unexpectedly 'chez Khashoggi' – this time with Nabila. We fondly remembered two years ago in Gstaad with Robin's dad and my mum. Plans had been made to visit friends in England, but as that was now impossible a special meal was prepared at the Villa. I felt very concerned because there hadn't been time for present-buying. However, Dan (our very understanding chauffeur) noticed my dilemma and offered to drive me secretly to a shopping-centre where I might find the coffee-machine I wanted to give to Robin 'on the day'. Driving me in his own Jaguar, he demonstrated his prowess as he no doubt broke every speed-limit. All was achieved, and I was able to surprise Robin with <u>two</u> gifts: a beautiful French coffee-maker and a superb leather belt. Nabila's gift still graces our main room in Eastbourne: a ceramic ornament depicting a clown and a wizard playing cards. If you look carefully you can see that they are both cheating! Our chef made a decorated cake, and Bertrand, our ever-attentive butler, took photos for us to send home. We really felt pampered and appreciated although away from our friends in England.

Saudi Arabia:

Once again – the unexpected happened, and a change of plan was organised. Our summer in London was not to be! It was felt by Adnan that Nabila was straying too far from her 'roots', and that a trip to Saudi Arabia should be arranged to include visits to her relatives and to Mecca itself. There she could perhaps absorb some of her ancient culture and learn to appreciate her widely-spread family. At Nabila's insistence we were invited to accompany her on this voyage of discovery, and after acquiring the necessary visas and undergoing detailed examinations of our passports, go we did!

May 6th: Jim Weeks again checked us in at Heathrow's Terminal Three, and off we flew in the DC9, accompanied by Adnan's surprisingly young step-mother, Um Amr, and Soufian Yassine who would co-ordinate all our affairs. Our in-flight lunch was lobster, steak and salad. When we landed in the Saudi capital, Riyadh, that evening we found several air-conditioned Chevrolets waiting to take us for a family meal. Many of Um Amr's relatives were there to greet us, and over a huge feast there was much discussion of family business, which seemed to be largely in furniture and shipping. With a temperature of 35 degrees centigrade it was a blessing to be indoors in a large house with full air-conditioning.

The following morning Nabila and I visited a Women's University where they were rehearsing dancing for an entertainment. Four of Crown Prince Fahad's ninety-nine daughters attended here, and many countries were represented in their celebrations, including Scotland. That evening we were at the Oasis Hotel for an engagement ceremony, and again it was all ladies. I was invited to join the feast of cakes, sweetmeats and drinks (no alcohol, of course). At 1 am. the only male entered: the bridegroom-to-be. I realized that the couple had met once only before, as all marriages were arranged by parents. They were now allowed to meet, chaperoned, but not in public until the day of their wedding. The ladies' hairstyles were beautiful and elaborate, despite the fact that Riyadh did not allow professional hairdressers as the trade was thought to be a cover-up for prostitution. A sheep-roast and many sweetmeats brought the evening to a close.

During our next two days there were several more visits. The first was to a modern (if oddly-named) Military Hospital. All of the patients were women, and I noted that patients were veiled when being examined by a male doctor. We were shown the latest equipment: no expense had been spared to ensure that every facility was available in up-to-date surroundings.

The Ladies' Bank of Saudi-Arabia was also on our list of visits. It was an eye-opener as it was run *by* women to enable them to conduct their *own* financial affairs. AK's offices there were magnificent, as was the hotel owned by Nabila's Uncle Adil (a brother of AK). Fitted with designer furniture, it was reckoned to be the best in Riyadh: it even had rooms with adjoining kitchens for ladies who did not wish to dine in the same room as men. The shopping complex was also superb, and Nabila bought me a cream Louis Feraud suit, the jacket of which I still have to this day. I had, of course, advisedly brought with me clothes which concealed legs and arms, but I noticed that nevertheless French and English designer clothes were all on sale, as many women needed to look fashionable on their frequent trips to Europe and America.

On May 13th we were taken on our DC9 for a flight over the most inhospitable desert - with oil wells and rigs - to land at Dhahran airport, Al-Khobar. From our base at the Hotel Algosaibi we went straight to see a beautifully-equipped modern school for girls aged 5 to 16. It was owned by a Princess, and the fees were 5,000 SR a year. Unfortunately Robin was not allowed to go: as a psychologist and lecturer in education he would have enjoyed seeing their amazingly up-to-date facilities.

The town of Dharhan is a piece of the USA dropped in the middle of a desert. Here we were *both* taken to see the American mixed school, and the golf-course smoothed not with grass, but with oil! Our visit neared its close at an exhibition showing the history of Aramco Oil, and finally a tour of a new, modern clinic. The two doctors who showed us round were very proud of what had been accomplished amid such harsh surroundings.

May 16th. and we were on the move again. Take-off was from the VIP lounge reserved for princes and visiting dignitaries. After a bumpy flight due to varying air currents over the mountains, everyone else was dropped off at Medina for a visit to Mecca. Not Robin and me: Moslem custom did not allow 'non-believers' to set foot on holy ground. It was, however, a welcome relief to be on our own for a brief spell. The all-English cabin-crew were happy to chat to us – something impossible when they were performing their flight duties.

Hussein, manager of AK's Jeddah establishment, picked us up at the airport. We were very glad of his services as we had been obliged to give-up our passports to the customs in Riyadh. Hussein clearly knew how to smooth our entry. And what a welcome we received from the staff who rarely saw visitors. A large, rambling house, garden and swimming-pool were at our disposal while the rest of the party were in Mecca for a couple of days. The pool was heated to a temperature that avoided undue bodily shock on immersion. We were proudly shown the many plants by the Philippino gardener, an expert horticulturalist. Juices were provided on arrival, and Lebanese chicken and salad made a refreshing supper. We swam in the cool of the evening, and took the opportunity to phone relatives in England to let them know where we were. No computers in those days! Forty-eight hours later we were off again.

Um Amr, AK's young step-mother, was with us on our trip and very anxious to visit her birth-place and relatives, so arrangements included a visit to Taif. We all had lunch on the plane, and in forty-five minutes landed in Taif, where we were to be driven to the Sheraton Hotel. The car journey there across mountainous terrain was horrendous, but the hotel itself was quite out of this world. Very cool, decorated in blue and white throughout with marble bathrooms and galleried public areas, all designed to create feelings of calm and leisure. We dined that night in the seventh-floor banqueting suite with magnificent views of the surrounding mountains. Unfortunately Nabila wasn't feeling too well, but recovered a little after taking some of my special medicine: we have learned never to travel without our 'jollop'. Rima, one of our party, was sent out on a shopping expedition for various feminine necessities and came back with enough sanitary towels and medication for the whole hotel! Apparently such articles are difficult to find in those areas, so she was making sure we were stocked up.

The swimming-pool was a delight, except that Robin and I were not allowed to swim together. 10 am – 2 pm was set aside for men, and 2 pm to 6 pm for women.

The next day a convoy of cars took us into a wonderful mountain area. Here we saw camels, Bedouin huts and large cultivated areas where farmers are given grants to maintain the land. To our eyes the countryside seemed somewhat barren, but our Arabic hosts clearly enjoyed revisiting their family roots. Our outing finished with a cheese-buying spree before we were all driven back to the Sheraton Hotel to collect our luggage, and then flown back to Jeddah. There we were welcomed by Hussein, and by Nabila who could hardly wait to tell us about her trip to Mecca.

The next few days in Jeddah proved to be the most relaxed spell in our entire Saudi experience. The residence was cool and spacious: the accommodation large enough for us to separate or to come together as we pleased. Particularly interesting to us and to Nabila was the arrival of two of her friends: Gerard and Eric Bertrand. (*right, with Nabila*). It was their habit to visit Saudi towns four times a year with examples of exquisite jewellery from their establishment in Geneva. Princes and princesses would invite them to their palaces or houses with a  view to buying or ordering their merchandise, and Nabila was clearly on their list. They were welcome guests as their cosmopolitan conversation and news interested us all. Their display of fascinating and extremely unusual rings, bracelets, etc., was quite dazzling, and Nabila succumbed to a pair of beautiful earrings. They were dined (not wined, of course) and swam in the pool while giving us news of what was going on in Switzerland. Obviously their regular visits to Jeddah and Riyadh were well worthwhile.

This leisure time gave us an opportunity to talk openly with Nabila: something she much valued as so many of her friendships were fleeting. Honesty and the ability to exchange *true* feelings were much appreciated: often the wealthy are told only what the speaker assumes they *want* to hear, not what they *need* to hear.

A few days later, as we were preparing for bed around 11 pm, every light went out, and we wondered what had happened to cause such a failure in their well-ordered world. It seems that something had gone wrong as new improvements to the electrical supply were being installed. This was serious, because the air-conditioning ceased, drinking water was no longer pumped, toilets could not be flushed, refrigerators stopped working, and no cooking or telephoning was possible.

We discussed what our response should be, then a car was hastily despatched to the hotel where our pilots and aircrew were staying during their 'time off'. They were told to report to the airport immediately and ensure that the DC9 was fuelled and ready to fly us all to Riyadh. Our complete household then proceeded by car to the airport. There was not time to take any luggage – some of us were in our pyjamas - but at 5.30am the luxury plane took off, We all felt rather like escaping refugees as we gazed down on the entirely dark city. Ironically, as we climbed to our cruising altitude, we saw all the lights of Jeddah click back on again, but the pilot's wise decision was that we should proceed to the capital where we were by now expected. The following day, of course, we all flew back again to Jeddah, where Nabila was able to confirm that her expensive new earrings and necklace were still safely on her dressing-table.

A few days later our Saudi-Arabian saga came to an end. There was some delay because AK had temporarily lent the DC9 to the President of Sudan. On June 7th, however, we took off homeward at 6 pm. Um Amr, Robin and I were reflecting on all we had seen, while Nabila was wildly excited at the thought of seeing her beautiful Villa and her dogs again after such a long period of time.

We landed to refuel in Crete, and arrived safely in Nice where, as ever, none of us had any customs formalities to undergo. We were driven to the Villa, where the dogs gave Nabila a boisterous welcome. We ate a superb meal by the pool, conscious of the intoxicating smell of cypresses and green grass, after several weeks in a wholly different climate.

Summer and Autumn in London:

It was difficult to adjust suddenly to life back in Lausanne. At Le Rosey School it was end-of-term celebrations, prize-giving and play presentations: could we get back there in time? We managed to see Hussein give an excellent performance as Demetrius in *Midsummer Night's Dream* with Chris, the drama teacher, in the comedy part of Flute. Once again Roger Moore was in the audience, this time to see his son as one of the Mechanicals. His talented daughter, Deborah, was with him in the audience. Malcolm Whitehead, the headmaster and his wife Judy invited us to dinner where they filled us in on many of the term's events. Mercifully all seemed to be going well.

Wednesday July 29th. How fortunate we were to be back in London at Roebuck House on Charles's and Diana's wedding day! From our apartment we had a perfect view of the whole proceedings: all London seemed to be excited and agog.

That was also an important time for our tutor Keith Warner (*right*). He dashed in to tell us that he had been called for interviews with Peter Hall and Lord Harewood, commenting that the fact that he had been 'tutoring the daughter of the Richest Man in the World' may have had some influence on their choice. Be that as it may, by August 31st he had been appointed Staff Producer at English National Opera. And he was then still only twenty-four!

By September Nabila was back in London with an idea that she might like to buy an apartment there as she was so enjoying the life-style of plays, exhibitions and music which we and Keith had opened up for her. It so happened that the penthouse in the very block where we were living was up for sale: could that be an ideal choice?

It was certainly impressive. One approached via a shallow marble staircase, and, once inside, the decor would have done justice to any Hollywood musical. The present owner was Cubby Broccoli (producer of the James Bond films) and the 'roof' of the large salon was in effect a sliding, domed solarium. Antiques and *objets d'art* from Somerset Maugham's house were displayed there: the whole effect was breath-taking. Asking price was one-and-a-half million pounds: a huge sum then. Of course, Nabila was interested, but there would be many bridges to cross before negotiations could begin.

That time was, by chance, a period when we could see practically the whole Khashoggi family together in London. Omar (Nabila's youngest brother) was suddenly rushed to the London Clinic for treatment. His mother (Soraya) and two of his brothers (Hussein and Mohammed) were all summoned to visit him. He recovered well from an operation on his lymph-glands, helped, no doubt, by the fact that his beloved Nanny and his close relatives were all there to boost his morale.

Visits and Visitors:
By September Soraya had decided to make a base in England, and Robin and I were invited to her lovely house in Goose Hill, near Newbury. It was good to see her again, and her beautiful little daughter, Petrina. Omar, her youngest son, was also there, enjoying 'helping' the chauffeur who was putting right some mechanical problem in Soraya's limousine.

Soraya had always enjoyed traditional Sunday lunch with Yorkshire pudding, and we were treated to that again. We laughed as we recalled the times when we were in Lausanne and she cooked this for Mohammed, her eldest son, on his weekends off from school. The recipe for Yorkshire pudding must be carved on our hearts! We spent most of the day in her lovely garden, reminiscing and discussing future plans, while we watched Omar playing 'big brother' with Petrina. Ironically, when it was time to leave, the chauffeur asked us for a lift into town where he could get some necessary parts for Soraya's car.

We were very pleased to see Debbie Nitke again; in London this time. By now she had become a very sophisticated young lady. She and Nabila arrived together one evening in stunning burgundy suits and hats. She was to join us for a season of theatre visits and art exhibitions, including productions of the ballets *Romeo and Juliet* and *Isadora* at Covent Garden. Richard Strauss's opera *Arabella* (with Kiri Te Kanawa in the lead) was also on the list, and fortunately Keith Warner was on hand to help us understand the complex story-line. By that time he was thoroughly enjoying life as a Staff Producer at English National Opera, and has since become one of the world's most sought-after opera directors.

We were a little bewildered one evening when Debbie told us of an invitation she had received from a charming young man whom she'd met at a recent party. He had, she said, invited her to join him and his family for a 'goose-hunting' expedition. She was tempted to say "yes" but asked our opinions. We requested further information, and, on hearing that the dates were to be in August we suddenly realized that what she had really been asked to join was 'grouse-shooting'. The young man's family turned out to be the Showerings who had grown wealthy by producing a then well-known and well-loved bottled drink called Babycham: low in alcohol, made from pears rather than grapes, and aimed at the female market.

The next day we were invited to Uncle Essam's house for lunch. Adnan's younger brother owned a very beautiful house called *Elk Meadows* in Iver, Bucks. He showed us round with obvious pride, and Robin asked him whether the building was genuinely old, or whether it was a brilliant copy. The reply made us smile: "Oh, it's genuinely old. It dates from the 1930s." To a Saudi man of the desert, I suppose that would make it genuinely antique. Essam's extended family made us most welcome, and proudly showed us the lake and park surrounding the property. We felt truly honoured to be included in this family gathering.

This seemed to be a month for comings and goings, as several visitors were welcomed at Roebuck House. Nabila had many friends and often gave invitations to people she had met and liked, almost implying they would be welcome to come at any time. On October 14th one such gentleman arrived in the afternoon. He was Jean-Pierre, a very good-looking young American. He stood expectantly on the threshold and told us he had saved up all his money for a transatlantic flight, just to see Nabila again. He said he felt sure she would be pleased to see him as she was so charming when they last met, when she had given him her London address. By now we knew she had made a number of other appointments, so it was suggested that Robin and I could perhaps take him on some theatre trips and other outings. I was sure that accompanying Robin and me was not exactly what Jean-Pierre had in mind; and this was proved to be a correct assessment when this by now rather forlorn young man, eating a delicious meal with us, could manage scarcely a bite.

I felt really sorry for him, and after much counselling managed to persuade him that with his personality and good looks there would be 'plenty more fish in the sea', and that Nabila was not going to prove his one-and-only. He was tearful, but when on October 20th he was supplied with a return-ticket to the States I could tell that he was 'sadder but wiser'.

Playwright and friend Christopher Fry was due to be in London when we were in Roebuck House with Nabila. He was supporting an art exhibition by Lorri Whiting, the wife of a friend of his. She had illustrated his poem *Curtmantle*, and her exhibition was in the Australian Embassy, no doubt because she was the sister of Australian Prime Minister Malcolm Fraser. Lorri was a keen yachtswoman, and her large pictures were all effectively seascapes. She was married to Bertie Whiting, a published poet who was a friend of Fry's.
All these connections provided an opportunity not to be missed: poetry, art and drama all gathered around our own dining table! We were not disappointed. We were among the first to know that Fry was making a four-part television film about the Brontes. It was a lunch to remember, and not just because they all appreciated my kedgeree.

Lamia and Dodi:

Once again it was to be Spring in Mougins. We were invited to Lamia's party in Cannes, and to meet Nabila's cousin Dodi Fayed who is also to be a guest. [Lamia (*right*) was Adnan's second wife.] We had bought a new car more suited to our needs: a Matra-Simca *Rancho*, which had plenty of room for luggage and higher suspension. Reviews had described it as a *Sheep in Wolf's Clothing*, because it looked like an off-road four-wheel-drive vehicle, whereas the only feature that was 'tough' about it was its shape. But we loved it, and after crossing the Channel on the mid-day Hovercraft we made for an evening meal and stop-over in Paris.

Next day saw us comfortably ensconced in Nabila's villa in Mougins - now fully furnished with a music-centre, a library and an open-plan dining-lounge area. Presents for Robin's birthday (February 12th) were waiting: a replica Royal State Coach and a beautiful book on opera. By the 5th we were sitting in the sun on the terrace, eating stuffed Loup-de-Mer, followed by peaches in apricot sauce. Coffee and cognac completed the meal. Could anyone have a better job than we had then?

We were curious to meet Dodi (*right, with Ann and Robin*) as he had often been talked of in fond terms. The son of Adnan's sister, with a father who owned Harrods and a mother who ran *Elle* magazine, he was clearly going to be an interesting young man. Quietly-spoken and extremely polite, he told us of his role as Executive Producer of the films *Breaking Glass* and *Chariots of Fire.* Over meals together during the next few days we heard of his military training at Sandhurst and his plans for the next possible film. He expressed a great admiration for England, with a love and understanding of all things English. His good looks and ability to anticipate one's every need made him a delightful companion.

February 12th, as in previous years, was to be spent with Nabila and her father. He called in to the villa for lunch, looking very fit and tanned, wearing blue-checked, open-neck shirt and light-blue trousers. After admiring the 'home improvements' he then dashed off again, saying he would see us all at Lamia's party. By now Hussein, Nabila's brother, had joined us: as a teenager he too took care with his dress and favoured outfits with a dramatic touch. Once again Robin's birthday was spent in wonderfully friendly and generous company.

Lamia's party was to be a much more lavish occasion. Hussein and Dodi, and then Robin, Nabila and I, were all driven by the ever-faithful Dan to AK's Cannes apartment. Set round an indoor swimming-pool, and surrounded by flowers, drinks were served to just twenty guests. A huge painting of Lamia (a present to her from Nabila) dominated one side of the main room. Lamia herself

 looked gorgeous in a Spanish-style black dress with red frills, her hair piled high to accentuate the necklace of rubies and diamonds with matching ear-rings. After many photos had been taken, dinner was announced, and we were all led down to the dining-room where five separate tables were set for the meal. A buffet fish-course of sole, lobster, shrimps and quenelles was followed by roast lamb, veal and beef, accompanied by many salads and vegetables. We were sitting with AK's personal physician, who revealed that he had had a quarrel with his wife, so she had not come to the party.

Also on our table was a fascinating lady whose English wasn't too accurate. She amused herself as much as us when she spoke of her visit to King Kong, when she meant Hong Kong.

Guests moved from table to table, chatting freely, until we were all ushered upstairs again for the cake-cutting ceremony. Many a camera clicked, of course; and then we all shared a very special treat: a Lebanese band struck up to accompany Lebanese dancers dressed in traditional costume. About 1 am. Dan drove us back to Nabila's villa where we spent the night. The followng day it was a long drive back to London, but Bertrand ensured we were not hungry along the way. Our picnic was big enough for six, and he had provided a full service of cutlery, plates and glasses.

Quo Vadis: Summer 1982:

It was time to take stock. After a career-break from traditional education of nearly five years we began to feel it was important to 'recharge our batteries' and investigate opportunities in England. Nabila was very anxious, after her time in London, to pursue a continuation of either her dramatic or literary interests; and AK's sons were seeking opportunities for further study in American universities.

We were asked to consider accompanying Nabila to the States for this next phase of her life. It was tempting, but we were aware that if we left it too long it would not be easy to return to good posts in English education. Reluctantly, therefore, we resisted pleas to continue acting as advisers to the children: this was a huge wrench as we had become part of the family: Nabila was almost 'the daughter we never had' but we felt impelled to start studying the Times Educational Supplement in the hope of finding posts in the UK to match our skills. I personally wrote some hundred job-applications and attended several interviews before accepting the headship of a village school in Buckinghamshire. When I set about re-focussing the mess which awaited me, and ordering new maths and reading-schemes, I soon realized that the county education offices were not nearly so generous as AK had always been.

The village was attractive, and the parents very co-operative: they seemed to appreciate that I knew what I was doing! We bought a house right next to the school, and decided Chearsley was probably where my working-time would end. We joined the local drama-group, made new friends, and got to know the area well. Two years later, however, I spotted an invitation to apply for a much larger headship in the attractive Sussex town of East Grinstead, applied, and was selected. We sold our house to someone who had children who would attend the Chearsley school, but hardly had everything been settled than the local authority decided the school was uneconomic and closed it.

So it was in Sussex that I completed some forty years in education. Robin continued occasional lectures on music and poetry before getting involved with the BBC: he was recording a music programme at Broadcasting House when we next heard from Nabila, and in October 1996 we saw her in London performing in John Cargill Thompson's play *Everything in the Garden*. It was a delicious reunion because she was beginning a career in the theatre and in films. In the audience was singer Shirley Bassey, a friend of Nabila's mother, Soraya.

Later, over in the USA, Nabila built a career publishing books for young people: specifically books encouraging concern for the environment. We have some of her best creations, the *Spartan and the Green Egg* series which aimed to teach children to cherish the world, and to protect it. Her theatre experience led to a short-but-successful career in Hollywood, and she is now married to millionaire James Cox Chambers and back once again in the world of high finance.

PART THREE

THE SUSSEX YEARS

The Sussex Years:

Frances Line.

Robin: A more recent stroke of good fortune came with our choice of Eastbourne for retirement. In 1991 I was invited to speak at the old Towner Museum and Gallery to celebrate the centenary of the birth of Richard Tauber. No problem, for I have upwards of a hundred of his recordings. The event seemed to go well, and afterwards a quietly-spoken lady from the audience asked if I had done any radio work. "A  little," I said, "on local radio in Sheffield and Derby". "Would you like a to do a programme for Radio Two?" The lady turned out to be Frances Line, the Controller of Radio Two: she had a holiday-home in Eastbourne and happened to be present at my talk. As a result I wrote and presented nearly fifty programmes about singers to far larger audiences than most music programmes get on Radio Three.

Was I a rather small 'somebody' at last? Many of the letters I received (to which I always responded) have brought lasting friendships.

Frances Line retired and now lives in the town permanently, so *our* friendship is a constant reminder of how much I owe her. Had we retired anywhere else I should never have enjoyed that luck.

Vilem Tausky, C.B.E. (1910-2004)

My first BBC Radio Two series was called *A Tenor Sang*, and as a result I was often asked to talk to some specialized group within which someone had heard and enjoyed what I was doing. I was in full spate during one such in London, introducing some of my favourite tenors of the past (on recordings, of course), and when I played a recording of the great Polish tenor Jan Kiepura, a little man in the front row jumped up and said, "I conducted his first performance in Czechoslovakia". For a moment I thought I should simply carry on, then I realized that we all wanted to hear details from the interrupter.

That interrupter was the great conductor Vilem Tausky. I spoke to him after my talk and he was so warm and encouraging that we instantly became friends, despite the difference in our ages. He's gone now, of course; but I feel I should document just a little of our friendship during his latter years. I see, in the Obituary published in *The Independent* on 24th March 2004, Graham Melville-Mason calls Vilem "this gentle, talented and remarkable man". From my experience I would say "Hear-Hear!" to that.

One of my favourite lecture venues was the Shell Centre at Teddington, next to the River Thames not far from Kingston in Surrey. A superb club, effectively a first-class hotel, for Shell employees. Occasionally, when I was earning an honest copper there, Vilem would turn up in my audience. Sometimes we would both stay the night, and sometimes Ann would be there too. He told her that he seldom ate breakfast, and then tucked into the full works. By then I think he had ceased full-time conducting and was living in a home for retired musicians somewhere south of London.

Though he never mentioned it, I learnt that this quiet, charming Jewish gentleman had been forced to flee the Nazis as they approached his home town. The escape involved organizing a mass-evacuation on a ship which eventually landed at Newport in Monmouthshire. For his part in all that he was awarded the Czech Military Cross. Arriving in Britain he was among those Czech servicemen who helped in Coventry after the dreadful night of bombing there. He had immediately composed his *Coventry Meditation* for string quartet.

After the War in Europe ended in 1945, Vilem discovered that many of his family had perished, so there was little point in moving back to mainland Europe. In 1948 he married an English girl whom he had met in 1940 and they settled here in Britain. His talent was swiftly recognized, and from 1945 to 1949 he was Music Director of the Carl Rosa Touring Opera Company. From 1951 to 1956 he was in charge of Welsh National Opera, and in 1951 made his debut at Covent Garden conducting Tchaikovsky's *Queen of Spades*. His career flourished.

Several years later Ann and I were invited guests at the Czech Embassy in London where he was to receive some significant award. I found myself sitting next to the Czech Ambassador, and we got into earnest conversation. He asked if I had ever been to Czechoslovakia, and I replied that I had been there when it was ruled by the Communists. "I was cleaning windows then" he said. "And what had taken you to visit my country?" I replied that I ran a small publishing-house and was about to release translations of poetry by a famous Lachian writer who lived in Bratislava. I went there in order to meet him. "Of course he is no longer alive", I said, adding that he wrote under the *nom-de-plume* Ondra Lysohorsky. "Lysohorsky!" he exclaimed. "We now regard him as one of the greatest of literary giants."

Vilem Tausky became even better-known to British audiences through his connection with the BBC Concert Orchestra's *Friday Night is Music Night*. In retirement in a residential home he had a close companion in Brenda Rayson who, coincidentally, we also knew well. She gave me Vilem's archive after he died, and she organized a delightfully friendly memorial service. I regard myself as being so fortunate to know that great man as a friend.

José Carreras (b. 1946, Barcelona)

When we were living and working in Switzerland we had an attractive apartment in Lausanne. We became aware, one day, that a tenor whom I had admired on the radio was to give a recital at the Palais de Beaulieu there. 8.30 p.m. on October 2nd, 1978. *Premier Récital en Suisse*. We immediately booked seats.

We were bowled over when José Carreras, certainly one of the most handsome tenors we had come across, walked onstage with his accompanist, Edoardo Muller. A glance at the printed programme indicated that it had been chosen with care. Bellini, followed by Schubert, with Rossini closing the first 'half'. After the interval we were to have Tosti, Meyerbeer, Verdi and Puccini. When he began to sing we realized we were hearing a lyric tenor voice of the greatest quality. No surprise, then, when the usually quiet Swiss audience called him back four times for encores. He used those opportunities to demonstrate his ability to be dramatic and popular as well as lyrical, with powerful songs *Granada*, *Amor te vieta* and *Core n'grato*.

During my time with Radio Two. I was assigned several different Producers: one of them suggested that I might interview a few distinguished singers who could speak reasonably good English. With him I set off to interview Carreras, who was in London for a popular recital at the Albert Hall that very evening. He greeted us warmly, and I began my opening remarks by recalling his Swiss debut, feeling quite sure that he would recall that triumphant evening in Lausanne.

80

He looked puzzled and asked, "Where was that exactly?" "The Palais de Beaulieu in Lausanne," I replied. I showed him the programme, and he said, "No, I don't remember it at all." Getting worried that this interview was going nowhere, I changed tack completely. "It has often surprised me," I said, "that so many great singers have come from your home town of Barcelona". His face brightened. "Ah, I would love to talk about that, but no-one ever asked me". At that he reeled off the names of several great singers who were born in Barcelona, and my interview went swimmingly from there on. I received many congratulatory letters via Radio Two, and plans were prepared for me to interview the other two famous singers who made up what had become known as *The Three Tenors*: Placido Domingo and Luciano Pavarotti. Luciano agreed to 'sit for me' when next in London, but on the chosen day he was unwell, so it never happened.

Barbara Fisher, O.B.E.

Barbara Fisher has lived in retirement in Eastbourne for many years. Her connection with music is longstanding: her first husband was a noted musicologist, and she herself was one of the country's H.M.I's, being herself a pianist of distinction. Her second husband (a retired Headmaster) was a talented painter, and several of his pictures grace our walls.

Barbara (*right, with Robin and singer Donald Maxwell*) has never been one to interpret 'retirement' as indicating "Do nothing" and remains a Vice President of the Yehudi Menuhin School, having until recently been the school's Chairman of Governors. Ann and I have enjoyed many a concert at the school, always aware that we are probably seeing and hearing a star of the future.

And talking of schools, "that reminds me"! Ann's third Headship was of a large primary school in East Grinstead. As such she was privy to a music festival that was being organised by (guess who!) Barbara. Ann recollects that she has never seen anyone else so able to hold spellbound some 300 children, all below the age of eleven.

Barbara's other great retirement passion is travel, and she often combines the two with trips to Vienna or Bayreuth. We consider ourselves privileged to have her among our greatest friends.

Brian Freeland (b. 1938)

We have known Brian for many years, and have become not only good friends, but admirers of his skills as a man of the theatre. Mention almost anyone of renown, and Brian will have a story about them. He always states that he is not an actor but, believe me, to hear one of his wonderful talks inevitably proves that he is no mean performer. Nor is he afraid  to take positions which go against conventional wisdom. I recall his saying that one of Eastbourne's beloved theatres should be knocked down and replaced with a modern, more efficient, building. That view did not please the majority but, based on sixty years of experience in all forms of theatre, it deserves consideration. Incidentally, Brian was Repertoire Manager at the finest repertory theatre I have ever experienced (Nottingham Playhouse) at the time of that world premiere of Christopher Fry's *A Yard of Sun*.

Brian is also no mean writer. I treasure his first book *Around the World in Eighty Plays* (2015) describing his adventures working in forty-three different countries. *Meanderings: A River and a Life* followed two years later, and his related illustrated talk about France's enchanting River Charente still lingers in the memory. His most recent book has the surprising title *Searching for my Tambourine*.

It is a wonderful display of what a life in the theatre really felt like, and en passant, reveals many, many surprising things about some other 'bell-ringing' names. I could hardly put it down, and still refer to it on occasion. I may say that where I have known personally any individual to whom he refers, I almost always agree with Brian's assessment that he/she is lovable or loathsome. I await his next publication with eager anticipation.

Beryl Grey, D.B.E., C.H. (b. 1927)
A note by Ann Gregory:

In the same way that *Orbis* introduced us to so many interesting personalities in Derbyshire, our involvement with the *Sussex Opera and Ballet Society* has offered further opportunities to widen our circle of contacts, with many of them becoming close friends.

In the *Sussex Opera and Ballet Society* we are privileged to have Dame Beryl Grey (*left with Ann*) as our Patron. As such she supports many of our functions, spending much time and energy on our various balletic interests. Robin is SOBS's President, so we are often seated at her 'top table' during the *Lunch and Listen* sessions, where her knowledge, expertise and lively conversation help the meetings go with a swing. Her immaculate wardrobe and impeccable bearing meant we all felt encouraged to 'stand up straight' and 'look our best' in her presence. From 1957 and into the 1960s Dame Beryl Grey was an international Guest Star, and the first English dancer to appear as Guest Ballerina at the Kiev and the Bolshoi Ballets. Later, under her direction, London Festival Ballet became the first foreign company to perform in China after the Cultural Revolution.

I particularly remember inviting her to an informal private lunch in our flat in Burlington Court, with four other musical/balletic guests. Robin was concerned that the remaining parking-spot might be difficult for her to negotiate, so he offered to drive her car in. "Indeed, No", was her reply, and she swept into the tight space with balletic skill. At lunch she was charming and relaxed, enthralling us all. Fortuitously one of the guests was Ieuan Roberts, teacher and pianist: they found that they shared many memories of past friends and musical incidents, and we all sat delightedly listening to their exchanges. Also present was Anne Dearle (a ballet pupil in later life) who found Dame Beryl a tremendous help as they talked of 'ballet for the older student'.

When I offered Dame Beryl de-caffeinated coffee at the end of the meal her response was "Oh No - *real* coffee please." Perhaps that was why, as she was leaving, she executed a perfect plié in our hall. There can't be many people who can claim to have had a private performance in their flat by Dame Beryl Grey.

Sir Edward Downes (1924-2009)
Remembered by Robin Gregory

The Guest Speaker at one of the formal lunches organised by the *Sussex Opera and Ballet Society* (SOBS) was Sir Edward Downes who proved to be a 'full-time nice guy'. My Radio Two programmes put me in touch with such opera stalwarts as Douglas Craig, former Director of Sadler's Wells Theatre. Douglas would occasionally travel down to Eastbourne for a SOBS meeting, and this was clearly one of those occasions since the archives include a notable photograph showing him with Anne Cleverton (then SOBS Chair-person), Sir Edward and Lady Downes, and me.

One happy memory of that occasion was that a SOBS member whom we had got to know well, Paula Allen, and Sir Edward greeted each other warmly, and we learnt that their friendship went back to the day when he accompanied her on the piano at her audition for a role with Carl Rosa Opera.

We last met Sir Edward when we were invited to the Albert Hall by Frances Line, Controller of Radio Two, to hear him conducting. There was no sign then that his sight was failing, and it was a good while later that we heard of the sad experience where he and his wife were so smitten by terminal cancer that they travelled to Dignitas in Switzerland for assisted (and legal) suicide. Alan Blythe, in his Guardian obituary of Sir Edward Downes described him as "Leading conductor of Verdi at Covent Garden and a stalwart champion of Prokofiev". While I would not disagree with that, I can say with confidence that his fame rests on far, far more. By the by: Paula (who sang as Pauline Allen) crops up in another coincidental meeting. We met her in Eastbourne, where we are both retirees, and got to talking about experiences in operatic audiences. I mentioned my particular love of the tenor voice and by way of example cited an occasion when I was in the R.A.F. and Ann was in her first teaching job at Havant. Spotting that *The Barber of Seville* was touring to Worthing we had made our way there. I had been so impressed by the unknown tenor that I jotted down his name, Kenneth McKellar, who shortly became a major star. That made Paula sit up, as she said, "And I was singing Rosina in that production on that very day". Small world, isn't it?

Ian Caley (b 1948, Preston)

Ian Caley was another of our Guest Speakers at the *Sussex Opera and Ballet Society*. I first met this international tenor at the home of a psychologist friend named Bill (R.B.) Joynson. Bill and I were fellow-members of the British Psychological Society (and I treasure my inscribed copy of his 1974 book *Psychology and Common Sense)*. Bill's wife sang in a choir that was about to present Handel's *Saul* and, having a sizeable home near the church

where the performance was to take place, they invited the soloist, Ian Caley (*left*), to stay the night with them. Ann and I also enjoyed their hospitality that evening, and met the young tenor for the first time. Ian tucked into a superb meal, showing no sign of nerves, and in the event he out-sang three more famous soloists. His mellifluous high, bright sound gave promise of a great career.

We heard him later as a perfect Gerontius, and loved his performances of such tricky composers as Janacek. He did indeed have a fine career, travelling especially to Europe, and singing in such operas as *Intermezzo* by Richard Strauss with Felicity Lott. He also had a great flair for operetta: I have never heard anyone sing the Pavilion Duet in *The Merry Widow* better. On LP his *Every Valley* from *The Messiah* is probably the best available. He has performed frequently on the radio, often with Marilyn Hill-Smith. Now retired from professional singing, he still does some coaching near his home in Harrow.

Jan Kiepura (1902-1966)
Marta Eggerth (1912-2013)
Marjan Kiepura (b. 1950)

As part of my first BBC Radio Two series *A Tenor Sang* I highlighted the great Polish singer Jan Kiepura who had, as a very young man, become a star at the Vienna State Opera. Imagine my delight when I received a congratulatory telegram from the United States, commenting that I had given the best broadcast the sender had ever heard covering Jan's starry career How, I pondered, had anyone in the States known about Radio Two, let alone been able to listen? The answer was that Marjan Kiepura (a successful concert pianist, and one of Jan Kiepura's sons) had been tipped off about my broadcast by his fiancée, who lived in England. I suspect she held the phone against the radio whilst I was 'on air.

Soon a correspondence developed, and I discovered that Marjan was coming to England. We arranged a lunchtime meeting at a hotel in Sevenoaks, Kent, where I learnt much more about this talented family. His father Jan Kiepura had been (rarely for tenors in those days) handsome and could act, and he soon became a star on film. There he was partnered by a particularly beautiful young Hungarian soprano named Marta Eggerth, and the couple fell in love. [The same process had brought Anne Ziegler and Webster Booth together in Britain.]

In March 1938 they fled Austria, taking refuge in the south of France. After the war they settled in the States, took American citizenship, and co-starred in many theatrical productions, most notably Lehàr's *The Merry Widow*. Alas, Jan died of a heart-attack at the age of 64. Martha lived to the age of 101, residing for much of that time with her son Marjan in the States. I was delighted to learn that Marta was giving an illustrated talk at the Wigmore Hall in London, and that Marjan (who would also be there) had reserved tickets for Ann and me. The hall was packed: both the Polish and the Austrian ambassadors were there. Marta delighted us all with her rendition of *Vilja* from *The Merry Widow*. Always the star, she circulated tirelessly at the reception afterwards, speaking to the many, many 'followers' who were in the audience.

One of my happiest moments was a transatlantic phone to Marta on her hundredth birthday. She was as spry as ever that day, but a year later the New York Times reported: *"Marta Eggerth - almost certainly the last living link to the grand musical confections of Franz Lehar and Emmerich Kalman, died on Dec.26th at her home in Rye, New York. She was 101."*

To glimpse the talent of this incredible family I suggest these CDs:-

Images of a Homeland:
Marjan Kiepura, piano, plays Chopin (Patria Productions)
Jan Kiepura, volume one:
 (Verdi, Puccini, Korngold, Stolz, etc. (Pearl)
My Life, My Song:
2 CDs covering Marta from 1932 to 2002. (Patria Productions)
My Song for You:
Jan Kiepura in solos, and duets with Marta. (Pearl)

Marilyn Hill-Smith, soprano (b. 1952)

One of the privileges of broadcasting on Radio Two was that one received complimentary tickets for *Friday Night is Music Night*. As Marilyn Hill-Smith was often the 'star' singer (106 times, would you believe?) on that 'live' programme it was inevitable that we should meet occasionally. I especially recall one occasion when she was singing a duet with quite a famous tenor when he suddenly forgot his lines. Without batting an eyelid, Marilyn simply sang his words until he caught on again. That's professionalism for you!

She has one of those exquisitely beautiful voices that can sing anything, often better than anyone else. The conductor Jane Glover recently told me that in her opinion Marilyn had retained that beautiful voice because she had the best technique in the business.

I recall Marilyn giving a recital at the old Towner Art Gallery in Eastbourne. She began with *One Fine Day*, the first note caressing the air, and the entire aria bringing tears to the eyes. From the radio I have recorded so many wonderful examples of her work: some of it with my great friend Ian Caley. From Lehar's last operetta *Giuditta* no-one can match her breath-taking *Meine Lippen sie Kussen so Heiss*.

I included Marilyn in my second Radio Two series, *A Diva Sang*. In my introductions I described her as "The best Viennese soprano to hail from the Home Counties". Coincidentally I think I was beginning my stint as a teacher at Cheam Sec Mod Boys School when Marilyn's mother was living in the same area. When Marilyn came recently to sing in Eastbourne, voice undimmed, I left a note at the stage door for her, and learned that she is now 'Mrs Daye'. A star – yes! And a lovely human being too.

Richard Lewis, tenor (1914-1990)
real name: Thomas Thomas

After Ann and I moved to Eastbourne, we got to know Elizabeth Muir-Lewis, a former operatic soprano who seems to know everyone connected with the arts, and who organises classical music concerts. Her husband Richard Lewis was a tenor whom I knew mainly from his records, particularly his superb *Gerontius*. I really looked forward to meeting him, even though by then he had suffered a stroke and was no longer performing. I decided that at our first meeting I would tell him a story about an elderly Derbyshire lady, a widow, whose husband had died only a few days after their marriage – killed in action in the Great War. A convinced believer, she told us how she had never remarried, despite several offers, because she wanted to be pure when the two of them met again in Heaven.

She became ill, and (convinced she would meet him again very shortly) she asked me to ensure that at her funeral the music should be Elgar's *Gerontius*, and that the performer should be Richard Lewis. I expected Richard to shed a few tears when I told him this moving story, but it didn't work out like that. He smiled and said, "And which of my two recordings did she prefer?"

Richard, I knew, was the only tenor who could have asked that question, as no-one else had recorded the role twice. My reply was factually correct: she wanted the recording conducted by Barbirolli. "Mmm", said Richard, "I had a bit of a cold when that recording was made, and I gave the better performance on the earlier recording with Flash Harry (Malcolm Sargent)". There, I thought, is a true professional!

Elizabeth, still frantically busy organising concerts and talks, has re-married: she and her present husband (Terry Pridmore) are among our closest friends.

Dame Felicity Lott, soprano (b. Cheltenham, 1947)

As a lover of fine singing, the name Felicity Lott has been ringing bells for me for many years.

I particularly admired the exquisite timbre of her voice, and knew she was no mean actress when I saw her sing the leading role in Richard Strauss's *Intermezzo* at Glyndebourne (and treasure a video of her playing in it opposite my friend Ian Caley).

Ann and I had been flattered by an invitation to become Governors of a school in Bexhill for children with behavioural problems.

Another of the Governors knew Felicity and had arranged for her to give an evening performance at the beautiful De La Warr Pavilion to raise funds for an extension to the school buildings.

After the arrangements were in place she found herself committed to sing a leading role in Vienna; many stars would have pulled out of the Bexhill commitment but Felicity would not hear of it and insisted on singing as promised. Thanks to my presenting duties on Radio Two, I was asked to be Master of Ceremonies.

On the morning of the concert I was making notes while she got to know her accompanist. Her usual pianist was unavailable, and David Willison was at the keyboard. It was a very happy morning until they rehearsed Schubert's *Shepherd on the Rock*, which is known to be a difficult 'sing'. One particular top note wasn't to her liking, and in my ignorance I whispered to David "What are we going to do about it?" He simply said, "She'll sing it all right this evening", and indeed she did.

Dame Felicity is now in semi-retirement, but takes great pleasure in talking about her career. When a BBC Radio Three morning presenter referred to the fact that she was to address the Eastbourne Recorded Music Society, and said "That'll only cost you a couple of quid as a guest" I arrived at the Church Hall that evening to see a queue stretching half-way to the gate.

She is also a Vice President of the Sussex Opera and Ballet Society, of which I am the undeserving President. I was asked to act as interlocutor when 'Flott' and her friend the great conductor Jane Glover were the guest speakers. All I had to do was to 'switch them on', sit back, relax, and enjoy the chat.

Robert Simpson (1921–1997)
Composer, writer, music-producer

Before retiring to Eastbourne Ann and I lived in a delightful village between Thame and Aylesbury. When, at the end of our 'Khashoggi Years', we decided to return to England we both assumed that our unique experience would guarantee swift re-employment in British education, but we were quite wrong. The British employers did not see our experience as valuable: they regarded us as "tainted by nasty foreigners". [We Brits can be very insular, as evidenced by the decision to quit our contacts with Europe and go it alone.]

We were invited to many interviews, but always placed below the experienced teacher 'just up the road'. Eventually, having filled in over one hundred job applications, Ann accepted a post in the little Buckinghamshire village of Chearsley, to discover that the Local Authority had made no evident attempt to clear the mess which passed for a classroom in their Chearsley School. Ann laboured away with no other qualified teacher on her so-called staff, and we took it for granted that Chearsley was the place from which she would eventually retire. Mercifully after two years she landed a large headship in East Grinstead, where the governors were actually seeking someone with her experience.

Chearsley itself was quite an upmarket little place with some very nice houses, one of which (right next to the school) we purchased. Our lovely neighbours soon became friends. One day we heard that there was to be a meeting just along the road to discuss the need for nuclear disarmament. I was told the large house where it was to be held was occupied by a distinguished composer which, indeed, proved to be the case, and I enjoyed my first meeting with the composer Robert Simpson. Also present were the son and daughter-in-law of Edmund Rubbra (1901–1986), another British composer. Tricia Rubbra, the daughter-in-law, had some beautiful pottery for sale, and I happily bought two matching mugs *to help the cause.* I still treasure them.

I confess that on that occasion I was not aware just how important the very-welcoming host was. Not only had Robert Simpson (*left*) composed eleven symphonies, four concerti and fifteen string quartets, he was also the author of authoritative works on Wagner, Beethoven, Bruckner, Nielsen, and Sibelius. He was so softly-spoken and gentle, that I can scarce believe that during WW2 he had served with an ARP mobile surgical unit during the London blitz, nor that for about thirty years (from 1951) he was one of the BBC's most respected music producers. I have a stunning recording of his Piano Concerto played by Piers Lane, with Barry Wordsworth conducting the BBC Concert Orchestra. Must play it again!

David Willison: Pianist/accompanist

I have already described my first meeting with David when he accompanied Felicity Lott at Bexhill's De La Warr Pavilion. He must have been satisfied with my 'presenting' on that occasion because, when he found himself in charge of the music festival in Rye (Sussex) where he then lived, he asked me to 'present' one of the concerts he had organised.

This was a recital by a beautiful young soprano, Judith Howarth, to whom I was introduced at David's home on the day of the event, and whom I came across again in 1997 when she played the name-part in the first (and only) staging at the Theatre Royal in Norwich of William Alwyn's superb opera *Miss Julie*.

David Willison was the regular pianist for Benjamin Luxon for some thirty years; an association brought to an end by the hearing loss which ended Luxon's singing career in the late 1990s. Since then Willison has established artistic associations with the violinist Ralph Holmes; the flautist James Galway; the Hungarian cellist Thomas Igloi; the mezzo-soprano Felicity Palmer; and the soprano Rita Streich. A significant recital and broadcasting partnership was also forged with the tenor Anthony Rolfe Johnson; this resulted in a number of recordings of English song.

David and his charming speech-therapist wife live in Faversham, Kent, in a beautiful property overlooking the Church. He has a number of pianos, each with a specific purpose. David and I share a love of American musicals and meet up at Chichester Festival Theatre whenever they include a musical in their summer repertoire.

David ran master classes in Eastbourne for a while. He was once asked to take over an exciting engagement at La Scala Milan when Gerald Moore found he could not make the journey to accompany Elizabeth Schwarzkopf. Her recital on that occasion ran to several encores, one of which caused her to tell David that she was "getting tired, and would he please put the final item down a semitone". Apparently that was an impossible request, so before a packed house he simply played in the correct key. Mme. Schwarzkopf was in an exceptionally good frame of mind and said, "I knew what you had done, and I was wrong to have asked you". That was an evening I should love to have heard.

Two of my treasured musical books are by Gerald Moore, widely accepted as the king of accompanists.

One was delightfully entitled *Am I too Loud?* (1962); the other was *Farewell Recital* (1978). David Willison gets a mention in the latter: a perfect quote to end on:

"The recital I anticipated with eagerness was Benjamin Luxon with David Willison. Only once did I play for Luxon: in the meantime I had heard him in opera, singing and acting superbly, but this was my first opportunity of hearing him in recital. His singing was masterly. He was partnered to perfection by David Willison, and Luxon recognized this."

That's it, then. You've now met virtually all our 'names which ring a bell': if you have time on your hands why not try doing something similar. Unless you already <u>have</u>, of course. As a favourite broadcaster used to say: "If you have been, thanks for listening." And do get in touch if we have rung any bells which you'd like to comment on. Meanwhile, au revoir.

Ann and Robin.

Eastbourne's Wish Tower and Coast: photo by Helen Elliott